DATE			
DEC 17 '80			

OUR
FEDERAL
GOVERNMENT:
How It Works

Also by PATRICIA C. ACHESON

America's Colonial Heritage

The Supreme Court

WE HOLD THESE TRUTHS TO BE SELF EVIDENT

OUR FEDERAL GOVERNMENT: How It Works

An Introduction to the United States Government

by Patricia C. Acheson

Illustrated with drawings
by Everett Raymond Kinstler

REVISED AND ENLARGED EDITION

Dodd, Mead & Company

NEW YORK

Library of Congress Catalog Card Number: 69-18462

Printed in the United States of America
by Vail-Ballou Press, Inc., Binghamton, N. Y.

Foreword

The federal government of the United States is vast and complicated. The very number of departments, agencies and bureaus which carry out its functions make an understanding of government difficult indeed. To understand, however, how it works, even in part, is important for all young citizens of this country. This book is an attempt to explain in brief what some of the major divisions of our Washington government are and how they function. To include every government agency would be an impossible task in a book of this sort. Selections, therefore, had to be made, but it is hoped that the young citizens who read this book will have a better understanding and knowledge of the organization and purpose of the federal government which has developed from the Constitution.

PATRICIA C. ACHESON

Contents

CONTENTS

1

The Constitutional Construction of the Federal Government

Why Have a Government?

Everyone everywhere knows that there is a federal government of the United States. Everybody knows that this government is located in Washington, D. C., and everyone grows up with the knowledge that the President of the United States lives in the White House on Pennsylvania Avenue in Washington. We all know also that at the end of that avenue, housed in a large and stately building, the Congress of the United States meets and makes laws for the people concerning all sorts of subjects. Some know, too, of the Supreme Court of the United States which is the guardian of all the rights of the American people and the highest court of justice in the land. Everyone certainly knows about taxes. But what does all this knowledge really mean? What does the government really do? Why does it exist? How does it affect the lives of all the American people? Why are taxes necessary?

Before the importance of what the federal government does, why it does it and how its actions affect the life of every citizen, can be made clear and have any real meaning, it is important to know and understand what government means, why we have government and what we must do to deserve government in the first place. The easiest way to decide what government in general is and to realize why it is necessary to have it, is to imagine what life would be like without any government at all.

Without any sort of government there would be no nation. There would be no American citizenship. There would be no patriotism, no Flag, no "Star-Spangled Banner." Without a government there would be no order to our lives. Each person would be alone and apart from his neighbors. No one would have any loyalty to anything other than his immediate circle of family and friends. All the things in our lives which we take for granted such as the Post Office or the Armed Forces, would not exist. There would be no protection against crime or unlawful actions either at home or abroad. We would be at the mercy of anyone and everybody. Strong people could take advantage of the weaker ones. In other words, without government life would be full of uncertainty and danger. No one could go about in peace and safety. We would be neither prosperous nor free. And above all, we would not be Americans because there would be no United States.

A nation, therefore, to be a nation, must have some form of government in which all the people living in that nation can believe and which they want to support. This belief in government and the willingness to support it makes each person, whether native or naturalized, a citizen of the nation, giving him certain rights and privileges and a sense of belonging to a group. Citizenship means loyalty and pride and respect for our Flag as a symbol of our nation. The existence of our government makes the United States an independent country and gives us as citizens individualism and a place in the world.

That, therefore, is what government means in the life of each individual living in our country. But there is something more to it than what it does for us. To have the advantages of government, each citizen must give in return something to that government. A country can be compared to a very large family. Each member of a family must abide by certain general rules in order to make the family successful. Each must share with the other members. Each has certain jobs and duties to perform to make the home a good one. So it is in a nation. Each citizen must fit into a general pattern, abide by certain rules or laws so that everyone can be sure of his rights and have freedom to live happily and in safety. As in a family, each citizen of our country must give up a bit of his personal freedom to do as he likes when he likes in order to make the country progress for the good of everyone. A topsy-turvy country would be to the advantage of no one. Government keeps our country from being topsy-turvy, but not simply because it exists. It keeps our lives from being chaotic because we as citizens are willing to respect our government, to work for it and to give up some of our individual, selfish freedom in order to make the government a success. A basic reason for any government at all, then, is to provide an organized system by which we can live as a nation in peace and prosperity. Equally important are two other reasons . . . to give us a voice through which all Americans may speak and to give us a sense of importance and individuality. For these ends government does exist and must exist.

The Writing of the Constitution

What is the government of the United States exactly? How and when did it come to be? Who were the people who agreed to accept our government and why did they want to accept it?

In 1783 the Revolutionary War was won by the Americans against the British. With that victory there had to be a new government for the thirteen States as all ties with England were, of course, ended. The big question was what kind of government should this brand new country adopt in order to preserve the freedom won by such sacrifice and hardship. The people of the American colonies had fought to free themselves from being ruled by an English king according to English law. They now wanted to have their own laws and to decide for themselves what would be the future of their own country. They knew that they wanted a form of government that would insure them basic liberties. Creating a good government, however, is by no means an easy task. The Constitution of the United States was not written right away, and indeed it could only come into being after another system had been tried and had proved to be a failure.

Because the citizens of the thirteen colonies had fought so hard to separate themselves from the rule of a king, they were afraid of the power of one man or even the power of a strong central government. When the thirteen colonies became independent States after the war, and the new Americans thought about a new government, they quite naturally believed that they would be more free if each State remained almost entirely independent of the others. The first government that the States adopted under the Articles of Confederation therefore gave more power to the individual States than to the central government. Each State had the right to coin money; each had the right to decide its own legal system; each had the right to defend itself. The central government consisted of a Congress made up of representatives elected from the States. Each State, regardless of how many citizens it had, could only elect two to seven representatives, but no State had more than one vote when it came to passing laws. There was no President with certain specific powers, only a chairman to keep order. As far as power to do anything went, the central Congress had very little. It could attend to relations with nations abroad. It could run the affairs of the territories belonging to the United States, but not those belonging to the States. It could try to settle differ-

ences between the various States should they arise, but there
was no well-defined system of justice to which all the States
had to bow. In fact, the list of what powers the central government did not have is a great deal longer than those that it did
have. The general Congress could not, for instance, pass tax
laws nor could it coin money for use by the States. To carry
out its activities, the members of the central government could
only politely ask for money contributions from the States. If
the States did not choose to help, then no money could be
raised. Because it had no money of its own, the central Congress could not pay any of its debts, and, indeed, it could not
even borrow money very successfully because who would lend
money when it was quite clear that it would not be paid back.

The Congress could not even raise an army or a navy to defend the new nation, because it could not gurarantee to pay the soldiers or the sailors. Very soon it became obvious that this system of government was not working out. Even the States, which had thought to give freedom and prosperity to their citizens by having this weak central government, discovered that there was neither freedom nor prosperity under this system.

Perhaps the worst problem that was causing so much trouble and confusion was that of money. Each State was issuing its own kind of money. Trade, therefore, between the thirteen States was very difficult. A man, for instance, in New Jersey crossing over into New York to sell his goods would discover that his goods were worth something different in New York than in New Jersey. If he sold them anyway, he found that the money he received for them was not worth much when he went home to New Jersey. Also, he might often discover that the State of New York was taxing him for selling his goods in New York. If the only market for his goods happened to be in New York, he was obviously trapped. He would never make much money as long as this system existed. This was typical of the situation all over the new nation, and the farmers and the businessmen were all suffering. In the colonial days trade had been brisk between the colonies, and everyone was now discontented.

This discontent and the fact that the new nation was extraordinarily weak without an adequate army or navy made thoughtful people realize that a better government must be worked out if the United States of America was to be a strong and rich nation. In Philadelphia in the year 1787 a meeting, or a convention as it was called, met in order to remold the government. It was there that our present system of government was born, and the Constitution of the United States was written. The people of the fifty States, the District of Columbia, Puerto Rico and the territories now in the Union are still governed today by the framework drawn up in that document despite the changes in America over the years.

The Preamble

Before working out a system for the new government, the men who designed the Constitution felt strongly the need to explain what an ideal government should be. In the first paragraph of the Constitution, called the Preamble, the ideals for a government dedicated to serve its citizens were carefully spelled out. The people of the thirteen original States knew exactly what kind of government they were going to have and why they needed such a government before they were asked to adopt it as their own.

The Preamble begins with the words "We the People of the United States." "We the People" meant exactly that. No one person or group was to accept the Constitution. The people of the nation who were going to be governed were the ones who had to agree to their government.

"In order to form a more perfect union" follows. "A more perfect union" was a direct reference to the less than satisfactory union established under the Articles of Confederation. The new government was to set up a union of closely allied States under a federal government instead of a loose confederation of semi-independent States. The States under this new union were to have their rights, but the union under the Constitution was to be strong and efficient.

In order to make this possible the founding fathers stated firmly the reasons for a good government in the Preamble. To

ERK

The Writing of the Constitution

be a strong and fine government, it must ". . . establish justice, insure domestic tranquility, provide for the common defense, promote the general welfare, and secure the blessings of Liberty to ourselves and our posterity." No nation can be strong without justice under law for all, without an army and a navy to protect its land and its people from foreign foes, without good, forward looking laws to help the individual citizens lead happier and richer lives, without the protection of the basic freedoms of a free, intelligent people. With these basic ideals written down at the beginning of the organization of their government, the people of the United States could have faith in their central government and a desire to live forever under its framework of laws.

The Constitution founded a democracy. The word democracy comes from the ancient Greek language. Demos means people. Kratos means strength or power. The two words together mean the strength in or of the people. A government based on democratic principles means a government in which the power rests in the people. They who are to be governed will form that government. They will be the ones who carry out the duties of that government. They will be the ones who will live under that government. Therefore, because the people of the United States are the government, that government must inevitably serve them. Should it fail to serve them, it is the people's right and duty to find out why it has failed and to correct whatever is wrong. In a democracy the government is only as good as its citizens, and, therefore, every citizen in a democracy must take responsibility and care about his government. The people of the United States have cared. Since 1789 when the first Administration under the Constitution took office the democracy set up by that document has endured. Many men and women of succeeding generations have lived under this government. All manner of problems, events and developments have taken place since 1789 changing the face of the United States, but still the Constitution remains virtually unchanged, commanding the loyalty and respect of the American people.

The Constitution

The Preamble stated the fundamental principles to be followed by the United States government. It now remained to translate these ideals into a practical system. How was the government actually to be "of the people, by the people and for the people"? How was it to "Insure tranquility, common defence, promote the common good and secure the blessings of Liberty for all"? The actual government must put the principles of democracy into working day-to-day democracy in the lives of the people. The machinery of the government must insure freedom, not only for the citizens of the United States in the eighteenth century, but for all times.

To create such a government was not an easy thing to do. Remember that in 1787 the men at the Convention in Philadelphia were pioneers in the setting up of a democratic government. They knew definitely what they did not want. They did not want a king. They also knew definitely that they did not want too strong a central government because they were afraid of losing their own freedoms. They wanted certainly to keep the States as they were. To erase them was impossible. Each colony had been founded for a different reason in the beginning, and each had individuality and pride. There could be no question of making just one government and forgetting the individual States. On the other hand, the men in Philadelphia knew all too well that the first government set up after the Revolution under the Articles of Confederation had been a miserable failure. It had had too little power to carry out its business. The States had bickered among themselves, and no one had been satisfied.

Here was a problem. On one side it seemed that a strong central government was bad. It might endanger the people's liberties. But, on the other, a weak central government had proven poor. It could not keep order, and the people were not able to make as much of their liberties as they ought to have. Americans since 1787 owe an everlasting debt of gratitude to those men who found the solution to this thorny problem. The system they worked out and wrote into the Constitution was the answer to the problem of how to have a democratic government to serve the people and to preserve their freedom, yet at the same time to avoid the danger of concentrating too much power in the Federal government. The solution they found is called the "checks and balance" system, and it is the heart and soul of the Constitution.

The Checks and Balance System

The framers of the Constitution wanted to make sure that the people's rights would always be safe and that the central or federal government would never become too powerful. A government to work most efficiently and democratically ought to have three major powers: to make laws, to carry out those laws and to provide justice under law for the best interests of the people. Should these three functions be in the hands of one person or one group, there would be great danger that that person or group could use the power for personal profit rather than for the people. To guard against this possibility, the Constitution provided for three major branches of government: the Legislature, or Congress, to make laws, the Executive to carry out the laws, and the Judiciary to watch over the rights of the people as described in the Constitution.

The powers of these three branches of the government are described carefully in the Constitution. The men in 1787 were so afraid of too much power in the hands of a few that they worked hard and long to spell out each job for the three parts of the federal government. Nothing was to be left to chance. To make sure that the government should never take more power than what it was granted in the Constitution, it was carefully stated that any power not given to the government should forever belong to the States. This remarkably foresighted decision meant that, although the country could grow from a little one into a great nation over the years, the rights of the people would never be absorbed by the federal government. If changing times caused new problems to arise, the States or the people had the right to decide what to do. No one branch of the federal government could simply assume the power and not answer to the people.

Another reason for describing carefully the powers of the three branches was to prevent any one branch from becoming stronger than the others. Each job in the running of the country was balanced between the Legislature, Executive and Judicial branches. The jobs were also intertwined. Each part of the government can only function in relation to the others. This system not only balances power between the three branches, but also provides a check on each branch by the others. For instance, a good example of the check system can be found in the manner in which laws become laws. The Legislature, or Congress, has the job of drafting laws for the country. Once a law has been passed, the Congress must send a copy of that law to the Executive, or the President of the United States, for his approval before the law actually becomes the law of the land. He may agree with the law and sign the copy in which case the law goes into effect. Or, if he should feel it is not a good law, he may veto it. Vetoing means that he refuses to sign. Should he do that, the copy is returned to the house of Congress in which it originated. If the Congress, sure that the law is a good one, passes it again by a two-thirds majority, the law becomes law regardless of the President's veto. The people are represented in the Congress, and if they still favor the law, it is more democratic that they should have it. The foresighted writers of the Constitution saw that there would be times when the people could disagree with the President. Should this occur, the people in a democracy must have the last word. That is the meaning of democracy. There is also a third possibility open to the President in the making of a law. He may ignore it and allow it to lie on his desk for ten days. Should he do this, he indicates his disapproval, but he does not veto it. After ten days that act becomes law, provided that Congress is in session. This course of action gives the Preisdent a chance to register an opinion between yes and no. At times it is very important that he should have the opportunity to say nothing rather than to be forced to agree or disagree.

The checks system goes further. The Judicial branch has its say about the law of the land. Once the Congress and the President have agreed on a law, it must be enforced all over the United States. Should someone disagree with a federal law and challenge it by breaking it, the case is brought into the court system of the United States. If the Supreme Court receives the case, it has the duty of examining the law and determining whether it is constitutional, or, in other words, whether the law is in keeping with the rights of the people as outlined in the Constitution.

This system of balanced power and of checks between the branches of the government means that at all times the people's rights and interests are being carefully guarded. There is no chance that a strong man or a group of men can take over the government and force the rest of the people to do their will.

The Three Branches of the Government

THE LEGISLATIVE BRANCH

The founding fathers had a deep belief in the people of the United States. They believed that government can only exist to serve the people. These beliefs are reflected in the Constitution. After the Preamble, the first Article of the Constitution is devoted to a description of the Legislative branch of the government, the United States Congress. Legislative means the making of laws. The laws of a country are of the greatest importance. If the laws are good ones, the people of a nation will live in peace and prosperity, but if they are poor laws, everyone suffers. Therefore, the making of laws for a country is a serious job. Because laws affect every person, the people in a democracy must have the right to make their own laws. It is in the Legislature, or Congress, that the voice of the people is heard. It is not surprising, then, that Article I of the Constitution sets up the Legislative branch.

The first sentence of Article I says that all lawmaking powers in the United States will belong to a Congress made up of a Senate and a House of Representatives. In other words, there shall be two sections of the Congress of the United States. In that simple sentence lies one of the most important and wisest decisions of the founding fathers. The decision to have two houses of Congress was not easily reached, and a great struggle took place in 1787 before the writers of the Constitution came to this agreement. The reasons for this struggle are threefold. For one thing, in 1787 life was very different than it is now in the mid-twentieth century. There were few schools and, hence, many people in the original United States had not much formal education. Some of the men in Philadelphia who cared deeply about good government worried that the privileges of democracy would be lost by giving too much responsibility to people who could not understand the difficult principles of lawmaking. Others felt quite the opposite. They said that unless all the people, regardless of their education, had a voice in the United States Legislature true democracy would not exist. They felt that, although the responsibility of making laws was a great one, the people would always be able to accept it.

The second problem which caused difference of opinion concerned how often the Congress should be elected. Some felt that frequent elections would mean a too rapid turnover and that the government would constantly be in a state of disorder. Others favored frequent elections of Congress—men to keep the lawmaking power close to the people.

The third point that caused argument was the problem of the unequal size of the States and whether they should have an equal number of votes in Congress. New York State, for instance, is and always has been a large State. Rhode Island and Delaware are very much smaller. If the federal Congress was made up of representatives elected according to the number of people living in a State, New York would obviously have many more votes than either Rhode Island or Delaware. This disparity was not just, and the small States felt strongly about this issue.

These three differences of opinion created, indeed, a hard problem because, when the argument started, the men were thinking in terms of just one elected assembly to make all the laws. After long and often angry debates, a solution finally appeared. Why not have two houses or assemblies in the Congress: one to be made up of two men chosen from every State regardless of its size to remain in office for a longer term (See 17th Amendment.); the other, to have members elected from the various States, the number depending on the number of people living in the State, and to have shorter terms in office? This solution was a compromise. Compromise means the making of a decision in which each side gives in a little to the other. Each point of view was satisfied, and out of this solution came the Congress of the United States made up of two bodies, the Senate and the House of Representatives.

The House of Representatives is the section of the federal government closest to the people of the United States. The men who go to the House, as it is called for short, are elected by the people of their State every two years. A Representative must be at least twenty-five years old; he must have been a citizen of the United States for at least seven years; and he must be a citizen of the State which he represents. In keeping with the nature of this body, the powers allotted to the House are those nearest and dearest to the interests of the people of the nation. A very important job given only to the House of Representatives is the right to start all the laws about taxes. The power to tax, or to tell the people how much money they must pay to make their government work, is almost the most important power in a government. The tax power must be jealously guarded and controlled. Should a government have a power to tax unwisely

The House of Representatives

or too freely, the people would suffer. It must be the people who decide how much the taxes should be. The people are the guardians against tyranny or dictatorship in this case. As it is the voice of the people, the House must have the power to begin the tax laws.

Another important task belonging to the House alone is the right to impeach the President of the United States. Impeach means to charge an individual with a crime. If the President should break his oath of office or fail to carry out the duties of his office, the House of Representatives charges him, much as a policeman arrests a person who breaks a law. Once again, this power was given to the House in order to give the people a way to protect their rights should a President dare to overstep the limits of his office.

The House also has the right to elect their own officers. The Speaker of the House is the chairman of the assembly, and he is elected by the members of the House each time a new Congress meets. Traditionally, the man elected is always the leader of the political party which has the most members in that particular Congress. Congress also has the right to make its own rules and to run its business as it sees fit.

Across the Capitol building from the House of Representatives sits the other section of Congress, the Senate of the United States. It is made up of two Senators from every state regardless of its population. The term of a Senator is for six years as against the two for a Representative. He must be at least thirty years of age; he must have been a citizen of the United States for nine years; and he, too, must be a resident of the State from which he is elected.

The Senate is organized differently from the House. Although the Senators may choose some of their officers, the President of the Senate is not elected by that body. He is always the Vice-President of the United States. The reason for this rule is to knit together the Legislative and Executive branches of the government. This keeps the two from operating completely independently of each other. The Vice-President, or the President of the Senate, does not normally have a vote. He only keeps order, but should there be a tie vote, he then has the right to break the tie by casting a vote. To provide for a President of the Senate should the Vice-President be ill or should he become President due to the death of the President, the Senate has the right to elect from its members a President Pro Tempore. This right keeps the Senate from ever becoming disorganized and means that it can always do its job.

The Senate, like the House, has its own special jobs shared by no other body in the federal government. It has the sole power to try the President of the United States should the House decide to impeach him. When the Senate is forced to sit as a court of law and decide whether the President is guilty or not, the Senate organization changes. The Vice-President steps down from his job as President of the Senate. In his place sits the Chief Justice of the United States Supreme Court. This substitution is another example of the intertwining of the three branches of the government. The trial of a President is of such a serious nature that the people should sit in judgment. The Senators, with their added years and longer terms serving their country, are the best suited for this big responsibility. The Vice-President cannot judge as he is second to the President, and it would not be right to force him to voice an opinion in a matter so close to himself and his future. The Chief Justice replaces him to avoid that situation and is in a position to give the President the fairest trial under law. Since the founding of the United States government, this right to impeach a President has only been exercised once, in the case of President Andrew Johnson who was acquitted by one vote in the Senate. Although it is to be hoped that no other President will ever have to face impeachment, the importance of the power to try a President is obvious. It is another safeguard against the possibility of executive tyranny and a protection of the people's right to be free.

Another of the Senate's special jobs is to serve as a check on the power of the President of the United States. The President has the power to make treaties with foreign nations, but they are not law until the Senate of the United States ratifies them with a two-thirds majority. This right acts as a brake on the power of the President to deal with other nations. He cannot bind the United States by any treaty with a foreign government unless the Senators believe it is in the best interest of all the people. The Senate must also agree to the choice of men the President makes to help him carry out the job of Chief Executive. Members of the Cabinet, federal judges, ambassadors and certain other top officials in the Executive branch must receive the approval of the Senators before they can accept their offices. This check on the power of the President is another example of the care with which the men who wrote the Constitution safeguarded the freedom of the people.

Following the outline of the organization and the separate powers of the Senate and the House of Representatives, the Constitution then lists the powers of the Congress as a whole. Congress shall and must meet by law once every year. To us in the mid-twentieth century, this provision seems to be an obvious necessity. How would laws be made and kept up to date if Congress, the lawmaking body, failed to meet? In the eighteenth century, however, the inclusion of this specific law providing for an annual meeting was of great importance. There were two good European examples which influenced the framers of the Constitution and made them aware of the necessity of requiring the meeting of Congress by law.

Perhaps the most important example had been set by the English people themselves. In the seventeenth century, not only had the usually law-abiding English fought a civil war and executed a king in order to have a firm say in the making of their laws, but they had had to depose another king forty years later and pass their Bill of Rights to insure this very point.

The other important reason for requiring that Congress should meet annually came from the example set by certain eighteenth century European countries. Some countries in the Old World, although they did have representative assemblies to help the kings make laws, did not have constitutions requiring those bodies to meet. They came together pretty much at the will of the monarch. If the king decided to make laws without the advice or assistance of his assembly, he could whether the people liked it or not. They had no legal way to force the king to call the representatives together. Therefore, the people were at the mercy of the king's whim. Such as the case in France before 1789.

The writers of the Constitution of the United States had no intention of providing a cause for strife in this new nation if possible. They were going to be certain from the start that the Congress, the assembly made up of the elected representatives of the people, would meet annually by law, thus preventing the President from ever governing single-handedly. Indeed, it would be impossible for the Chief Executive to govern alone because the Constitution does not grant him the right to make any laws at all.

Originally, the Constitution said that Congress was to meet each year on the first Monday in December, but in 1933 that date was changed to the third day in January. (See 20th Amendment.) So, on that day each year the many Congressmen and Senators return to Washington from their various homes to begin a new session of Congress and to resume the responsibilities of lawmaking.

25

The work of Congress is controlled closely by the Constitution. The fundamental powers are carefully spelled out. Each house has the right to organize itself, to determine the way in which it shall do its business, to see that its members are properly elected, to punish them for bad behavior and to expel, if necessary, any member by a two-thirds vote.

Both the Senate and the House must keep a record or a journal of its debates which is printed by the Government Printing Office and is available to the public. The *Congressional Record* is a day-to-day record of the affairs of Congress. Only discussions which touch on matters which for the people's good should remain secret are not printed. Otherwise, anyone who is interested may follow the course of the making of laws and may find out exactly what his Senator or Representative is doing at all times. The keeping of an open record is another means of insuring democracy. Each voter has the right to check on his Representatives in Congress at will.

The Constitution not only describes the duties and responsibilities of the Congressmen, but also grants them certain protections and immunities while in government service. They are to be paid for their services by the United States Treasury. This decision to give a salary to the Congressmen paid by the central government was a wise one. Obviously the men coming to Washington must live while they are serving their States. Many would not be men of private means and could not afford to give up their jobs at home if they were not paid for their time in Washington. A federal salary guaranteed to the people that men of all backgrounds could offer their services to the government and not only those with wealth.

Congressmen were also guaranteed freedom from arrest while pursuing their duties in Congress. Naturally, major crimes, such as treason or murder, would not go unpunished, but one important result of this privilege granted to members of

Congress is to guarantee their right to express their opinions freely while either in the Capitol or on the way to and from it. Laws which grow out of free discussion are always better laws than those resulting from limited debate. No man should be penalized for giving his opinion in the course of doing his duty. Therefore, it is another safeguard to democracy to have the lawmakers at liberty to speak their minds.

The Constitution then goes on to list the responsibilities that Congress must bear. The list is exact. The fear of losing the people's freedom was ever present. To give too much power to the federal government of the United States would perhaps endanger the States and the people's rights. The original thirteen States, which were the bodies that formed the central government, wished only certain lawmaking powers to be granted to the federal Congress. The powers or rights not listed specifically in the Constitution belonged automatically to the States. This check on the power of Congress keeps that body from interfering with matters that are strictly the States' affairs. The powers listed as belonging to Congress are those which affect all the people of the country equally and are important to the peace, the safety and the prosperity of the nation.

The powers relating to money and to financial affairs that are granted to the federal Congress are of great importance. No government is a good one if it is not sound financially. It is not surprising, therefore, that the list of the powers of Congress relating to money is an impressive one. Congress, and Congress alone, has the right to coin money and to fix its value. Also, the punishments for counterfeiting or copying the currency of the United States are to be fixed by Congress. This central control over the currency of the nation was of great importance in 1787. Before the writing of the Constitution each State had its own currency, and confusion prevailed. Now every State and its citizens could do business easily with one legal form of money everywhere.

The right to decide the amount of federal taxes and to collect them belongs solely to Congress. If money is to be borrowed by the United States government for any reason, only Congress can give permission for the loan to be arranged. Commerce, both between the States and with foreign nations, is regulated by the Senate and the House of Representatives. These powers enable the federal government to regulate trade for the benefit of all the people in the nation and to keep commerce on an orderly basis.

Equal in importance to the financial responsibilities of Congress is its duty to provide for the defense of the country. Congress has the job of creating an army, navy and, in the twentieth century, an air force for the protection of our land. Although the Executive branch actually runs these departments, it is Congress which supports them by appropriating money annually from the general revenue of the United States and which keeps a constant check on the state of our defenses.

Closely allied with the power to provide for defense, Congress must also by constitutional dictate in an emergency decide whether or not this nation shall declare war. The President, if he thinks war is unavoidable, must ask Congress for a declaration. The President cannot act alone in a situation of such seriousness to the welfare of the nation. The people's representatives must agree before the safety and the security of the country can be jeopardized. Since World War II, however, the United States has made certain international commitments which have resulted in her participation in conflicts which have not been declared according to the words of the Constitution. By joining the United Nations in 1945 the United States pledged to protect member nations from aggression, and, therefore, in 1950 when the frontier between North and South Korea, which was guaranteed by the United Nations, was violated by the North Koreans, the United States together with other members of the United Nations fought an undeclared war until 1953 when it was terminated by negotiations. Again, a few years later, the United States found herself engaged in another undeclared war in Vietnam because of an international commitment, in this case her membership in the Southeast Asia Treaty Organization. When the Senate ratified the United Nations' Treaty and the Southeast Asia Treaty, the United States automatically accepted the responsibilities of membership, and the necessity of using force to enforce the principles of those treaties was one of the responsibilities. If no international commitment were involved and a nation were to attack the United States, the President, if he had time in this nuclear age, would, of course, still be required to go to Congress and to ask for a formal declaration of war.

Congress has many responsibilities other than defense and finance. It must establish post offices and post roads to enable the citizens to communicate with each other and to travel safely within the boundaries of the country. Congress also is given the power to encourage the development of arts and sciences. By issuing patents and copyrights for inventions and artistic works, Congress protects the individual from having his discovery or creation used by others and grants him any financial benefits derived from his idea for a given period of time. This kind of protection encourages men to contribute to the progress of the whole nation.

In line with keeping the country up-to-date, Congress also has the responsibility of creating more federal courts under the Supreme Court should they be required. As the country grew from thirteen States the need for more courts grew, and Congress, because of this foresighted clause, could add to the federal Judiciary, thereby insuring the right of trial of federal cases to all the people whether in the East or the far West.

The knowledge that the United States would grow resulted in Congress being empowered to regulate the naturalization laws for the whole country. Naturalization means the becoming of an American citizen of a person by birth the citizen of a foreign nation. As people from other nations were pouring into the new nation in the western hemisphere, there had to be a system for making them Americans. Congress must set up those laws and see that they are uniform throughout the country.

Having decided the powers that Congress had to have to make the new nation strong, the writers of the Constitution still worried about the possibility of the federal government becoming too powerful. They then made a list of all the things that Congress might never do. This list is of equal importance with the list of Congress' responsibilities because it reinsures the freedom of the States and their citizens and prevents the federal government from becoming dictatorial. Congress can never suspend the writ of habeas corpus except in cases of extreme national emergency. Habeas corpus is the law forbidding the imprisonment of any individual without a specific cause. The writ of habeas corpus is one of the greatest safeguards of liberty in that it protects the rights of an individual before the law.

Furthermore, Congress can never pass a law relating to criminal matters that would apply retroactively or to the past. All criminal laws, in other words, take effect at the time they are passed and cannot refer to a time or a person before that date. The power to tax is restricted also. Congress is expressly forbidden to tax any articles exported from any State, and no preference can be shown for one State over another in any commercial way. A last restriction placed on the powers of Congress is that never can that body create or bestow on an individual any title of nobility. This particular restriction seems to be very eighteenth century in its concept, but had it not existed, the citizens of the United States of the twentieth century might well not be each others' peers.

At the end of the long list of powers and responsibilities of the Legislative branch of the government, there is one last instruction to Congress, to find a suitable site for the capital of the United States. The Constitution was written in the old colonial city of Philadelphia, and the first city used as a capital was New York. There had to be a permanent home for the capital, preferably a new site to be established for the sole purpose of housing the federal government and to be governed solely to this end by Congress. The Constitution instructs Congress to find such a place or a "district." Several years after the establishment of the first government under the Constitution, Maryland and Virginia consented to give up some of their land, and out of this territory the District of Columbia was formed. From 1800 to today Washington, D. C. has been the nation's capital. The same clause granting Congress the right to rule the home of the federal government also granted Congress the right to take land for the use of the government for forts, arsenals, dockyards and the like. All federal land in the United States is governed by the Congress of the United States, just as it governs the District of Columbia, unless the government makes a special arrangement with the State in which the land is located.

The organization, duties and responsibilities of the Legislative branch of the federal government were thus carefully worked out. No detail was omitted in the attempt to create a working Congress able to carry out its functions, but at the same time restricted from ever becoming too powerful. Although the government has changed in some respects and expanded greatly in size, all the powers allotted to Congress have been carried out since the first House and Senate were elected.

THE EXECUTIVE BRANCH

Laws are a basic necessity to the democratic way of life. Therefore, the making of laws is a vital function in a democracy. If those laws, however, are not carried out, they would be of no value whatsoever. The job of carrying out laws in a democracy is of great importance. Who should be responsible for the carrying out of the laws enacted by the Legislature?

This question was a serious one to the people of the late eighteenth century in the newly created United States. The thirteen colonies had waged a long and expensive war against the arbitrary rule of one man, a king. Immediately following that war, the colonies had created a form of government without a central executive empowered to carry out laws and had found that system to be unsatisfactory. The answer to the problem of how to carry out laws had to lie between the two extremes. There should be neither an arbitrary ruler nor no ruler at all, but a President with carefully specified powers and a limited term in office.

Article II of the Constitution describes the Executive branch of the federal government in great detail. The Constitution places the Executive power in the hands of a President. To guard against the possible tyranny of one man, the President's term of office is limited to four years. No matter what the situation, every four years an election is held to fill the office of the President. A President can run for reelection if he so chooses, but he must run and be reelected to remain in office. He cannot simply stay in the White House because he likes it. In the original Constitution there was no limitation placed on the number of terms one President might have. In recent years, however, the people of the United States decided that it was better for the country to limit the terms to two. In 1951, the Twenty-second Amendment was added to the Constitution restricting any future President from being elected more than twice.

Who shall be elected to the Presidency and the manner in which he shall be elected were carefully specified in the Constitution. Anyone aspiring to the highest office in the land must have been born in the United States, and he must be at least thirty-five years of age. To insure the fact that his interests really lie within the country, the Constitution also demands that the candidate have lived for fourteen years prior to his election in the United States. The framers of the Constitution wisely realized that only a man whose life was centered in the land of his birth could be best suited to be the Chief Executive.

The importance of the job of President is so great that the manner in which he is elected had to be devised with care. Before the system of how the President is elected can be understood, it is important to remember the differences between the eighteenth century United States and the twentieth century nation. Communications were poor in the eighteenth century. There were few newspapers, no telegraph, no radio and no television. It was difficult, if not wholly impossible, for residents in one part of the country to know well people from far-off sections. Citizens could vote for their Congressmen intelligently because they came from local districts, but it was questionable if they could vote intelligently for one man whom they had no way of knowing personally. Because communication and transportation were so poor, the framers of the Constitution worked out a system for the election of the President that involved the election of a group of men from each State whose sole task it was to elect the President of the United States. These men who are elected to choose the President are called Electors. They have no other task than to meet following their election and, in turn, to elect after careful examination of the candidates the man they consider best suited for the presi-

18th century ✦ ✦ COMMUNICATION ✦ ✦ 20th century

dency. The people of the United States, in other words, do not elect their President directly. They vote on election day for men whose judgment they respect who then actually elect the President. To avoid confusion, however, the names of the presidential candidates appear on the ballot above the electoral candidates. The voter is certain to cast his ballot for the Elector who favors one specific candidate.

Today the electoral system seems very archaic or outmoded. With radio and television and rapid transportation by air or by land, every citizen knows the presidential candidates well. He has every opportunity of knowing them before the election by reading newspapers, seeing newsreels either at the movies or on television, or hearing the campaign speeches themselves on the

radio or television. The electoral system, however, still exists and will continue to exist until the Constitution is changed or amended. Although in recent years there has been much talk about amending the electoral system, at the present time no action has been taken to change it.

Although the Constitution lays down certain rules as to the age, nationality and manner of election of the President, it specifies nothing as to the individual's political beliefs. When the Constitution was written, there were no organized political parties in this country. George Washington, the first President under the Constitution, was elected unanimously by the Electors purely on his personal record, not because of any political affiliation. But today the President of the United States is the head of his political party, and he is elected by Electors who are chosen because of their political allegiance. In fact, a candidate for the presidency only becomes a serious contender because he was chosen by his political party. The reason for this difference is because it was not until after Washington's first election that political parties were founded.

In a democracy in which freedom to think and to speak are basic rights of each citizen, a political party is a natural development. Men are very vocal as to how their government should be run and what policies are good ones. That there should be differences of opinion in such a broad and important field is only natural. Out of these differences of opinion, political parties were born. Men who agreed tended to band together apart from those who held opposite views. These groups as early as the end of the eighteenth century became organized into what we call parties and began to play a significant role in American government. (See 12th Amendment.) The first party conventions, or meetings of the members of the party, were held in 1831 for the express purpose of selecting a candidate for the presidency of the United States. Since then the fact is that the President of the United States has always been a member of a political party, but nowhere in the Constitution is a political party mentioned. The parties were not planned; they just happened and have become an integral part of American political tradition.

Whoever he may be or to whatever party he may belong, the President of the United States has certain powers and responsibilities, and he must abide by his oath to carry them out. Every President, following his election, must be inaugurated before he can legally take over his job. The Chief Justice of the United

1 7 8 9

States Supreme Court administers the oath of office to the President-elect. He swears on the Bible in front of the American people to "faithfully execute the office of President of the United States, and . . . to preserve, protect and defend the Constitution of the United States." Once he has taken the oath he is the President and for four years must carry out the responsibilities of his office and the law of the land.

His job as President is carefully outlined in the Constitution so that there could be no chance of his taking over any powers belonging to either Congress or to the States. He is the Chief Executive of the federal government. He is the Commander in Chief of the Armed Forces and of any State Militia should it be called into federal service. This responsibility is of great importance. In history many a military man with the power of the armed forced behind him had taken over the government of a country and ruled by might rather than by right. The President of the United States is a civilian, and the fact that he is in supreme command over the generals and admirals of the Armed Forces serves as a guarantee against any military dictatorship in the United States. Should a military man be elected President of the country, he must resign his commission and command before taking the oath of office. He is elected as a civilian and remains one in the White House despite his past profession.

The President is entrusted with the job of appointing all men who serve their country as ambassadors, ministers, consuls, judges of the federal bench and all other officers of the United States. Before they can take the oath of their office, however, they must be approved by a two-thirds vote of the Senate. This restriction checks the power to appoint just anyone to a position of responsibility. The man chosen must be acceptable to the people. Should the Senate not be in session, however, the President can fill vacancies in order that the work of government may go on uninterruptedly, but the appointees must be confirmed as soon as the Senate reconvenes.

As the Chief Executive of the land, the President also has the power to grant pardons and reprieves for crimes committed against the United States. He may not exercise this power in cases of impeachment. In other words he could not pardon himself or anyone else to whom he gave office. This power to pardon is an important one in the meaning of justice. If the law demands the death penalty for a proved offense in a court of law against the United States, a judge is forced to give it as a sentence. If, however, the criminal has some valid reason to beg for mercy, it is the President's privilege to grant it if he sees fit. Mercy is a basic tenent of democracy, and it is important that the Constitution recognizes it by granting the President the right to exercise it.

Because the President is the Chief Executive and responsible for the condition of the nation, he is also required by the Constitution to report to Congress or to the representatives of the people on the state of the Union. At this time he not only reports on the state of affairs, but also suggests and recommends policies to Congress which he thinks advisable for the good of the country. In this way, the President becomes a policy maker. As the political party system in the United States has developed, the President's State of the Union address has become the traditional way in which he asks for the laws by which his party's platform, or campaign promises, can be enacted. Congress does not have to follow the President's suggestions or heed his requests, but the speech is a guide to what the nation's leader thinks should be done. The State of the Union address is traditionally presented in person by the President in the Capital at the beginning of each new Congressional session in January. This major address is followed by special messages from the White House to Congress dealing with specific problems confronting the nation.

The President is also required to ask Congress for a declaration of war, should he feel it unavoidable. He also has the responsibility for the making of peace treaties at the end of hostilities. This power is limited because the Senate of the United States has to agree to the treaty by at least a two-thirds vote. The President, therefore, cannot decide the question of either war or peace single-handedly. The Congress of the United States must be consulted and agree before such important issues can be settled.

All the Executive power and responsibility are vested in the President of the United States. Constitutionally no one may share his authority. But what if the President should die or become totally incapacitated within the four years in which he is the supreme authority? To prevent a complete breakdown of the Executive department, the Constitution provides for a Vice-President who shall become President in case of the latter's resignation or death. (See 25th Amendment.) Little has been said about the Vice-President in this discussion because unless he should become the President of the United States he has only one Constitutional role. He is the President of the Senate. Until very recent times the Vice-Presidents were the forgotten men of Washington. Although they are elected in the same way as the President by the Electoral College, they have no authority beyond the presidency of the Senate, and in many cases they remain simply unknowns for four years. In a few cases the "unknown" has been catapulted into the forefront of public life by the death of the President. Recently, with the world so full or unrest and tension, the Vice-President has been given more jobs by the President. He has important positions to do with national security and has become a regular member of the Cabinet, something he never even attended before. It is of importance that the Vice-President should be up-to-date with government affairs and be aware of the job of President in case of sudden death or severe illness flinging him into the White House. But any present duties of the Vice-President are those allotted to him by the President, not by the Constitution. He is hardly mentioned in that document.

The Constitution places squarely all the responsibility for the Executive Department upon the shoulders of the President of the United States. Should he actually break his oath of office, he can be impeached by the Congress. Should he fail in responsibilities, the people can elect another man at the end of his term. All during his term of office he is under not only the great pressure from work, but he is also under the scrutiny of the citizens of the United States, and he is the target of all who disagree with him politically. He cannot even move about freely, but is surrounded at all times by a phalanx of Secret Service officials. No wonder that the President has been called the loneliest man in the United States.

THE JUDICIAL BRANCH

The third branch of the United States government is the Judiciary. The functions of the federal court system are many. The Supreme Court is the arbiter in disputes arising between the States. It deals with cases involving controversies in which the United States government is a party. It may take cases involving ambassadors, public ministers and consuls. Greatest of all its functions, however, is its responsibility as guardian of the rights of the American people guaranteed by the Constitution. In this guardianship capacity lies the tremendous importance of the Judicial branch as the third and necessary part of the United States government.

The Legislature makes the laws; the Executive carries them out; the Judicial branch determines the constitutionality of those laws. Without a Judicial branch the United States would

not have the final check or balance needed to control government power to insure democracy. The federal Judiciary provides the ultimate guarantee of freedom. Laws can be made by the Legislature with the best intentions in the world to benefit the people. They can be carried out by the President with his sincerest conviction that they are good laws. But, if, despite the care with which they are framed, laws should turn out to endanger the liberty of any person or peoples or to be against the intentions of the Constitution, the citizens of the United States can turn to the Judicial branch of the government for redress. It is this privilege of seeking justice in the federal courts that guarantees democracy in this country. The Judiciary is the third and vital branch without which the United States government could not operate. As long as the federal courts exist, the rights, privileges and freedoms of the American people will exist also.

To carry out this vital responsibility the framers of the Constitution in 1787 stated that there should be one Supreme Court of the United States and provided for the establishment of other inferior courts as and when they were needed. This provision allowing for the expansion of the federal court system was another illustration of the wisdom of the writers of the Constitution. In 1787 there were thirteen States, but there was a vast country to the west. The founding fathers knew that the United States was bound to expand and with added States there would also be added need for more courts. Justice is lost if cases cannot be settled in a reasonably speedy time, and over the years more courts under the Supreme Court were made necessary by the increase in size and population of the nation. The Supreme Court is the highest court in the land and the final recourse in law. The district courts, the inferior courts, established in the United States since 1787, do not substitute in any way for the Supreme Court in Washington. They undertake to try cases acceptable in the federal system initially. The United States Court of Appeals decides questions raised in appeal from a decision of the district courts. The Supreme Court only accepts certain classes of cases from the district courts or the courts of appeals. Once the Supreme Court has decided a case, that decision becomes final, and all in the land must abide by it.

It is true, however, that due to changes in American life brought about by the passage of time, circumstances and different personalities on the Court, Supreme Court decisions have been reversed, and the law changed. As situations and conditions change, new interpretations must and do occur. At a given time a decision may seem correct and a good one. Many years later the same situation may arise again; the plaintiff brings the case to the Supreme Court. The constitutionality of the issue is therefore reexamined in the light of the present. If the judges see just cause for a new evaluation of the facts, they may arrive at a new decision, automatically reversing the decision reached about the same problem before. There is no such thing as static justice, and the power to reevaluate is a vital one to the democracy we value.

The federal judges, who must bear the responsibility of maintaining "Equal Justice Under Law," are appointed by the President of the United States. They hold their office for life and can only be removed for bad behavior. The purpose of life tenure is to make the federal judges and justices of the Supreme Court dependent in no way upon the power of political favor of Congress or the Executive branch.

The Constitution does not specify the number of men who shall sit on the Supreme Court. The number has been set at eight justices and one chief justice by Act of Congress. The Chief Justice is the head of the Court and beyond his regular judicial duties, the Constitution also requires that he preside over the Senate in the place of the Vice-President in the case of the impeachment of the President of the United States.

The Judiciary system of the federal government is one of the great bastions against tyranny. Since the establishment of the United States government under the Constitution, the Supreme Court and the inferior federal courts have steadfastly stood guard against injustice. Housed in a classic marble building close by the Capitol of the United States, the Supreme Court does indeed represent the firm belief of the American people that to live under law is to achieve and preserve freedom.

The Three Branches of the Government

Thus does the Constitution describe the organization and powers of the federal government. On close examination, however, it becomes clear that the Constitution actually draws up an outline for the government. Important and basic ideas are incorporated in the document, but there is no attempt to spell out or to explain the details of how each of the three branches must carry out its job. Only general patterns are laid down; for instance, Congress must legislate on a variety of subjects, but the method by which this legislation is to be arrived at is omitted. The President also is indeed responsible for many specific tasks, but again the way in which he is to accomplish these satisfactorily or with whose help is not specified. The Supreme Court is given certain definite powers, but it, too, has leeway in that it can decide which cases it will hear and leave others to the inferior federal courts.

The genius of those who wrote the Constitution lies in their willingness to believe in change and their unwillingness to impede the free development and progress of the nation by imposing crippling restrictions and limitations on the methods used by the three branches of the federal government in the Constitution. Had that document been more than an outline, the country would have soon found that it had outgrown the Constitution and would have undoubtedly discarded it. The flexibility and elasticity of the Constitution has meant that for close to two hundred years the country could be governed by the pattern set forth in 1787.

One specific article in the Constitution is devoted to the principle that change is necessary and good. Article V describes the methods by which the Constitution may be amended. The power to amend the outline of the government has kept it as alive and as meaningful today as it was in the eighteenth century. There are two ways in which an amendment can be made to the Constitution. By a two-thirds vote both houses of Congress can propose an amendment, and, if the proposal is passed by three-quarters of the State Legislatures or by conventions called in three-quarters of the States, it becomes a law and part of the Constitution. The States may also propose changes if two-thirds of them so desire by requesting that Congress call a convention to draft an amendment. If the proposed amendment is passed in the above manner, it also becomes a law. The systems of amending the Constitution are sufficiently complicated to prevent any irresponsible changes. In the many years in which the Constitution has existed, only twenty-five amendments have been added. The first ten were drafted and adopted in 1791, or almost immediately following the ratification of the Constitution by the original States, and are called the Bill of Rights. These amendments specifically guarantee certain rights and privileges to the American people.

We owe the Bill of Rights to Thomas Jefferson primarily. His first reaction to the Constitution when he read it was one of dismay. Where were the inviolate rights of the Americans specifically mentioned? Nowhere in the body of the Constitution could he find guarantees against the infringement of certain basic liberties. He felt that the form of government was useless without rights and privileges being included. His clear reasoning influenced many, and as soon as the Constitution was ratified, the Bill of Rights was drawn up and adopted.

The other fifteen amendments have been added over the years as changing times and conditions have demanded new laws. Prior to the Civil War only twice was the original language of the Constitution altered. The Eleventh Amendment, ratified in 1798, removed one type of case from the jurisdiction of the Supreme Court because experience had proved that its inclusion had been a mistake. The Twelfth Amendment, 1804, was a result of the growth of political parties. In the Constitution as it was originally written the runner-up for the Presi-

dency automatically became the Vice-President. After political
parties were established, it was impossible for the losing candidate to be Vice-President so the Twelfth Amendment directed
the Electoral College to cast two separate ballots for the two

offices. Following the Civil War three amendments were adopted dealing with the great changes brought about by that conflict. The Thirteenth Amendment abolished slavery, the Fourteenth defined the rights of citizenship, and the Fifteenth granted universal manhood suffrage. The remaining ten amendments all reflect the great social, economic and technological changes of the twentieth century. The Sixteenth legalized the federal income tax, and the Seventeenth provided for the direct election of Senators. The Eighteenth prohibited the manufacture, transportation and sale of intoxicating beverages, and the Nineteenth granted women the right to vote. The Twentieth changed the dates of the opening of Congress and the inaugura-

tion of the President and Vice-President. The Twenty-first repealed the Eighteenth, the nation having found national prohibition most ill-advised, and the Twenty-second, as mentioned above, restricted the number of terms a President may serve to two. The Twenty-third gave residents of the District of Columbia the right to vote for President and Vice-President, and the last two to date, the Twenty-fourth and Twenty-fifth, ratified in 1964 and 1967, outlawed the poll tax in federal elections and arranged for the Vice-President to take over presidential powers in case of the President's disability. That only one of the twenty-five amendments has ever been repealed testifies to the wisdom with which the amendment power has been exercised and how reasonably the Constitution has been updated.

The privilege to amend the Constitution is not the only way, however, in which that document has proved flexible. As the nation has grown in size and entered more importantly into world affairs, many government changes have taken place. Any of the writers of the Constitution, even George Washington himself, would be overwhelmed by the workings of the United States government today and would hardly recognize it to be the one they designed so long ago. Many of the ways in which the business of government is carried out today were never conceived of by the men of 1787 nor is there any mention of them in the Constitution. Washington is full of departments, agencies, bureaus and offices whose existence we do not question, but which were never mentioned in the Constitution. Their legality is made possible by the foresighted language of the framers. Congress has developed the committee system under the constitutional power "to determine rules of its proceeding." Congress has also passed laws about subjects not specifically listed in Article I, under the clause granting Congress the power "to make all laws which shall be necessary and proper for carrying into execution the foregoing powers, and all other powers vested by this Constitution in the government of the United States, or in any Department or Officer thereof." There are also now under the supervision of Congress many offices whose existence was never described in the original outline.

The Executive branch has also changed almost beyond recognition. The responsibilities of governing the country have grown so tremendously since 1789 that the President now requires much more assistance in order to be able to do his job. Whereas in George Washington's day the Cabinet numbered three, today it numbers fourteen. There are also many special assistants to the Chief Executive and advisory groups attached to the White House. Each new position or group has been created in answer to a specific need, and the expansion of the Executive branch has made it possible for one man still to be President.

All these extra-constitutional additions to the federal government have become traditional and as much a legal part of the government as though they had been part of the original pattern. Had it been so limited as to prevent the actual working of the government, the Constitution would have been indeed a sorry attempt at a lasting framework. As it was, though, the foresighted authors of the Constitution made room for the expansion of the government and therefore enabled the country to be governed practically and efficiently over the years.

2

The Growth of the Federal Government since 1787

2

The Growth of the Federal
Government since 1787

The Development of the Executive Branch

The Constitution demands that the President of the United States bear the responsibility for the Executive branch of the federal government. The President, and the President alone, must answer to the American people and to Congress for the Executive policies and actions. Nowhere, however, does the Constitution declare that the President must actually do all the work in the carrying out of his job alone.

From the first Administration the Presidents have been surrounded by men in an advisory capacity, some officially responsible for a particular department and others simply close friends of the President's who advise him unofficially. The President's "official" family today consists of the Vice-President, the twelve heads of the departments, and the United States Representative to the United Nations. These individuals make up the Cabinet. The White House staff and certain White House advisory groups are referred to as the President's "unofficial" family because, although they are appointed by the Chief Executive, they do not require Senate confirmation. Not one of the positions on the White House staff nor in the Cabinet is mentioned in the Constitution, but they have all been created over the years by Congressional authority to fill needs as they have arisen. Although the prestige and influence of the President's advisers can be great, it must never be forgotten that at all times it is the President who is responsible for all actions taken by anyone connected with the Executive branch of the government.

The President's staff works in the White House offices in the west wing, so that its members are immediately available at all times to the President. Their homes are also in direct contact with the White House as each is equipped with a special telephone hooked up to the White House switchboard. The men who fill the staff jobs are generally personal friends of the President's and assist him in various ways to carry the burdens of the office. They have no responsibility to anyone other than to the President himself. The members of the staff act in general as go-betweens. They maintain close liaisons with the Executive departments and agencies, the Congress and with individual Senators and Congressmen. As a general rule each assistant is assigned a subject for which he is responsible. National security affairs, education, health, science and technology, and communication are a few of the areas of responsibility. Much of the assistants' time is devoted to drafting speeches for the President and collaborating on messages to Congress suggesting legislation. At any given moment the special assignments of the President's staff reflect the subjects of particular importance facing the nation. There is no set number of assistants, each President having as many as he feels he needs. They must be prepared to do whatever the President wishes at all times, and, in spite of the fact that the job is terribly exacting, it is always challenging.

Also included in the White House staff is a Press Secretary and several assistants whose sole job is to see the press and to issue statements from the White House for publication and news coverage on television or radio. Again, the Press Secretary's job is unofficial. The developments in the field of communications have led to the necessity of having a full-time Press Secretary. In former years before the newspapers and elec-

The Press Secretary conducts a press conference

tronic means of communication were as highly developed as they are today, the President was interviewed once in a while by newsmen, but there was no problem. Today with reporters representing radio, television stations, newspapers and periodicals from all over the world demanding White House news, the President simply has to have a man whose time is devoted solely to this end. The power of the Press Secretary is great. His releases are the sources for the information presented to the American people and, indeed, to the world. It is up to him what to say, how much to say and how to say it, all of which gives the Press Secretary a good deal of authority.

Other members of the President's staff are a military aide, a doctor, a counselor, and a large secretarial group. The military aide represents the Armed Forces. At special functions, diplomatic receptions, presentations of medals, dinners, etc., other members of the Armed Forces assist in various ways, and it is considered a great honor to be chosen for the White House detail. The doctor is on call twenty-four hours a day and is responsible for the President's health which is of vital importance to the whole country. The secretarial staff handles all the White House clerical work, correspondence, documents, memoranda and the like. The counselor, with several assistants, acts in an advisory capacity along with the special assistants.

One of the more recent developments within the White House is the greater role in national affairs played by the First Ladies. They, too, have had need for a staff, and, apart from secretaries, a housekeeper and household help, they have been assigned an assistant who deals with the Press and a social secretary. These aides are also generally close personal friends and are responsible for any task that the President's wife sets. Gone are the days when the First Lady was expected simply to be a gracious hostess. Her changed role reflects the general acceptance and indeed expectation that women have responsible jobs beyond those of wife and mother.

The growth of the White House staff over the years illustrates the growth in the size of the presidential task. It would be absurd to imagine that one mortal man could attend to all the presidential responsibilities alone. The staff performs a vital function in studying problems, reading voluminous amounts of material, preparing memoranda for the President and keeping him up-to-date on all the many problems with which he is confronted. It must never be forgotten, however, that the staff is purely a work-saving organization and no member can ever take over any of the Executive authority. The President is the man elected to the White House by the American poeple, and all Executive actions must be taken by him.

Other White House Groups

Other White House Groups

The problems affecting the government of the United States which have arisen in the twentieth century are of such a vast nature and of such complexity that over the years it has been found necessary to create many more advisory groups to help the President with his task of running the country. Located in the Executive Office Building next door to the White House are the Bureau of the Budget, the Council of Economic Advisers, the National Security Council, the National Aeronautics and Space Council, and the Office of Science and Technology. The office of Emergency Planning, the Office of the Special Representative for Trade Negotiations, and the most recently established Office of Economic Opportunity are located in nearby offices because the Executive Office Building has no further space. There is a certain fluidity to these groups in that they are created to answer a particular need, and, should the situation change, then so does the group. The Office of Emergency Planning, for instance, replaced the Office of Civil and Defense Mobilization when it appeared wiser to move most of the latter's function to the Department of Defense. Each of these groups is directly responsible to the President, and, with the exception of the Bureau of the Budget, serves only to advise him in detail on the specific problems within its jurisdiction. When he has all the facts and suggested courses of action before him, the President is then in a position to make policy decisions in the best interests of the people.

The Bureau of the Budget performs a different function from the purely advisory groups. This Bureau was established in 1921 and was then placed in the Department of the Treasury. In 1939 it was relocated and made part of the Executive Offices of the President. The Budget Bureau has two functions: one, to prepare an annual budget for the Executive branch of the government, and, two, to work on the improvement of management and organization of the Executive branch and to act as a clearing house for any proposals for legislation coming from any of the federal agencies and departments. In other words, the Budget Bureau has both an advisory and a specific function. A budget is a necessity for any well-run business or even a home. The Executive branch of the government must have money each year in order to function. Each government department or agency prepares a statement asking for the money it thinks it will need for the coming year. These reports are submitted to the Director of the Budget. He and his staff go over them with a fine toothcomb to see that each item listed is really necessary. He usually manages to trim the estimates considerably before preparing the final budget which he submits to the President. The President then sends the budget to Congress whose exclusive power it is to appropriate the money to pay the bills. Tax laws can be adjusted every year in order to raise the cash needed for government expenditures. The budget goes to the Congress early in the calendar year, and Congress hopefully acts before the end of June. The government's fiscal year runs from July 1st to June 30th. Occasionally the fiscal year comes to an end before Congress has acted on a particular agency's budget, and, until the appropriations are passed, the agency has to live on emergency funds, cutting its programs to the bare minimum.

In the Budget Bureau's other capacity the Director advises the President on the reorganization of Executive Offices or agencies and on any ideas coming from the departments for laws perhaps necessary to their functions. The President, if he thinks the proposed legislation good, includes a request for it in either his annual message to Congress or in one of the many special messages he sends to the Capitol during the early months of the year. The close liaison between the Director of the Budget and the White House is another way in which the President is kept in touch with the vast machinery of the Executive branch. The Director of the Budget is appointed by the President and is one of the most important men in Washington.

The purely advisory offices of the White House function generally in the same way, but each of their responsibilities is different and illustrative of the complexities and problems of modern American society. Since the Great Depression of the 1930's no Administration had been unaware of the importance of gauging the state of the nation's economic health. The Council of Economic Advisers was first formally established in 1946. Three members serve at one time on this Council, and they are appointed by the President and confirmed by the Senate. Their chief function is to study the national economy, to evaluate the government's economic policies and programs, and to advise the President on ways to stabilize as well as to advance national prosperity. The National Security Council dates from 1947, reflecting the international tensions and insecurities in the aftermath of the second World War. The Council is made up of the President, who cannot always sit, the Vice-President, the Secretaries of State and Defense, and the Director of the Office of Emergency Planning. Its function is to collect and to integrate all material, foreign, domestic and military, relating to the nation's security. This clearing house enables all other departments and agencies of the government to act together more efficiently to make the country secure in these uneasy times. The Council with the correlated material at hand then advises the President on security matters. This information enables him and the Cabinet to deal to the best of their ability with the vital problems of national preparedness and security.

Under the National Security Council, although physically located about nine miles from the White House in nearby Virginia, is one of the most important agencies that has been added to the Executive office of the President, the Central Intelligence Agency. Before World War II the United States had no effective system of central intelligence. Whereas the British had for many years a Secret Service devoted to the collecting and sorting of intelligence reports, the United States simply had intelligence officers in each of the armed services and in the foreign service of the Department of State. Without a clearing center there was much needless duplication and no coordination. During the second World War it became apparent that the United States needed such a center, and the Office of Strategic Services was set up under the Executive wartime powers. In the postwar years this temporary agency developed into a permanent one, Central Intelligence. The purpose of the agency is to collect and to coordinate all the intelligence activities of the United States government. The evaluated information is then used to advise the National Security Council. Central Intelligence also helps the existing intelligence agencies in other government departments if they should request aid. Also the agency is prepared to perform any function relating to intelligence asked for by the National Security Council. The establishment of the Central Intelligence Agency is an excellent example of the way in which the Executive branch has grown and must grow to keep the nation abreast of world developments. Had the Constitution placed restrictions on the power of the President to create new offices, the federal government could not have survived the challenges of the twentieth century.

The National Aeronautics and Space Council and the Office

of Science and Technology quite obviously are the children of the incredible scientific revolution of the past decade. The Aeronautics and Space Council, set up in 1958, is chaired by the Vice-President and its members are the Secretaries of State and Defense, the Administrator of the National Aeronautics and Space Administration, which directs the nation's space programs, and the Chairman of the Atomic Energy Commission. The Council's principal tasks are to advise on the policies and plans of the space programs and to determine which of the many United States agencies engaged in space activities should be responsible for the many phases of the national space effort. It serves also as a clearing house and general coordinator. The Office of Science and Technology, established in 1962, has its own staff and is charged with advising the President and the Secretaries of the departments on ways to implement the new developments in science and technology most effectively for national welfare and security. They analyze the effects of modern scientific and technological advances on national policies and try to forecast major disruptions that might result from these new developments. The staff also maintains a close relationship with the scientists and engineers in the private sector, encouraging them to participate in programs by which to strengthen the development of science and technology in the free world, as well as in the United States. Thirty years ago no one could have possibly foreseen the need for these two offices, and yet at present with the speed with which science is progressing in all fields they both perform indispensable functions for the President and the nation.

The Office of Emergency Planning and the Office of the Special Representative for Trade Negotiations are the least known or publicized of the White House offices as well as the smallest. The chief function of the Office of Emergency Planning, as its name suggests, is to provide for all contingencies in case of an enemy attack. The Director is responsible for plans for the emergency use of all the nation's resources—manpower, transportation, communications, materials, industrial capacity, etc. He also plans rehabilitation programs for the citizens and the economy after an attack is over. This office is a direct result of the nuclear age, and, although it is hoped that such plans will never have to be tested, it is obviously wise to have the government ready in the event of such a disaster. The establishment of the Office of the Special Representative for Trade Negotiations resulted from the Trade Expansion Act passed in 1962 which empowered the President to change certain tariff rates without Congressional approval in order to increase trade between the United States and abroad. The Special Representative is appointed by the President and has the rank of ambassador. His chief function is to assist the President in carrying out all the provisions of the Trade Expansion Act and to advise him of all the non-tariff barriers to international trade and commodity agreements. This job may not sound particularly vital, but trade and its expansion is of great importance to the United States as Europe becomes more competitive now that her industries have been entirely rebuilt since the second World War. The importance of the job is illustrated by the appointment of a former Secretary of State as the first Special Representative.

The most recent and unique of the White House offices to be established and purposefully left to last in this discussion is the Office of Economic Opportunity. This office was created by the Economic Opportunity Act of 1964, the purpose of which was "to eliminate the paradox of poverty in the midst of plenty in this Nation by opening to everyone the opportunity for education and training, the opportunity to work, and the opportunity to live in decency and dignity." Unlike the other White House offices, the work of the Office of Economic Opportunity touches the lives of many people daily across the nation, and its function is to carry out programs rather than to advise. The Director of OEO and his assistants supervise six major antipoverty programs: 1) the Youth Programs, including the Job Corps, the Youth Conservation Corps and the Work Training Program; 2) the Urban and Rural Community Action Program, including the Adult Education Program; 3) the Employment and Investment Incentives; 4) Work Experience Programs; 5) the Special Rural Poverty Programs; and, last, 6) VISTA—Volunteers in Service to America. To assist OEO by coordinating all the resources of the federal government which are necessary in fighting the war on poverty, there is an Economic Opportunity Council composed of the Director of OEO, the Secretaries of Defense; Interior; Agriculture; Commerce; Labor; Health, Education and Welfare; Housing and Urban Development; the Attorney General; the Administrator of the Small Bussiness Administration; the Chairman of the Council of Economic Advisers; and the Director of Selective Service. The Office of Economic Opportunity in Washington is solely administrative and the actual programs are carried out in the cities, towns and hamlets in almost every State of the Union where poverty exists. The activities of OEO are so numerous and diverse and its programs so new and revolutionary in concept that it is too soon to evaluate its progress. The establishment of the Office, however, is another illustration of the way in which Congress and the Executive respond to a problem of national significance and attempt a solution.

George Washington or Abraham Lincoln would hardly recognize the office he once held, it has changed so much over the years. Although many deplore the size of the Executive offices at the present time, it is hard to imagine how else the President could execute his job. The world is too complicated for anyone to expect one man or a small group to cope with all the problems. It is unrealistic to think that the country could be run efficiently without the assistants and the advisory groups that surround the President. In spite of all their help and advice, however, the President's work load appears to grow heavier and heavier, and there is no question that his job is the most exhausting, demanding and yet exhilarating one that a man could have.

The Executive Departments

Whereas the offices, bureaus and agencies surrounding the President have been created almost entirely in the twentieth century, the creation of the Executive departments began with the first administration of George Washington. The Executive department heads, or the Secretaries, make up the President's official family, the Cabinet. The Secretaries of the Executive departments are appointed by the President, but they must be confirmed by the United States Senate before they can take office. These positions are purely political, and when the President's administration goes out of office, so do the Secretaries. Should the President wish to replace a Secretary, he may. The man or woman only holds the office at the President's will.

The affairs of the United States are many, and each department is responsible for a separate facet of the nation's life. The function of the Secretaries is to advise the President on problems relating to their specific department. Today there are twelve Executive departments, the first three dating from the early days of the Republic, the twelfth from 1967. The Cabinet consists of the Secretaries of State, Treasury, Defense, Justice, Post Office, Interior, Agriculture, Commerce, Labor, Health,

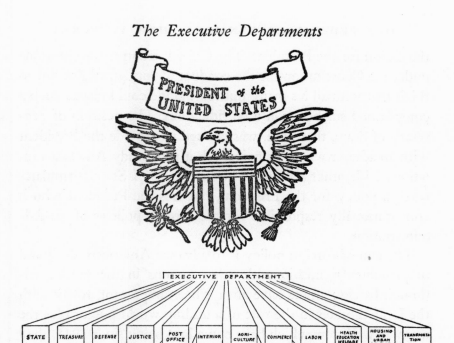

Education and Welfare, Housing and Urban Development, and Transportation. As the necessity arose, Congress would enact legislation creating the Cabinet post. Although each was founded for a specific reason and was granted the power to deal with a specific side of the nation's life, each of the Executive departments has changed and grown over the years to be able to cope with the changing life of the United States.

THE DEPARTMENT OF STATE

Under the government of the Articles of Confederation the foreign affairs of the United States were determined and carried out by a Department of Foreign Affairs. In 1789, after the adoption of the Constitution, Congress reorganized that department and created the Department of State. From that day forward the State Department has handled all the foreign affairs of the nation for the President. The Chief Executive is responsible under the Constitution for the conduct of foreign affairs, but to think that with all his many duties he alone could master such a complicated subject would be ridiculous. The position of Secretary of State, therefore, was created to provide the President with an adviser whose principal job it is to study America's relations with other nations. The Secretary of State formulates foreign policy for the President, but it is the President who is constitutionally responsible for the foreign policies of his Administration.

The aim of foreign policy is to advance American ideals and to promote friendship with other nations in the world. Although foreign affairs have always been important, today with the United States in the role of a leading world power plus the many new factors which have come into being since 1945, they have become extraordinarily complicated. The uneasy peace following the war, the clash of opposing political and social ideologies between the greater nations of the world, and the explosion of new nations out of former colonial possessions across the earth have profoundly altered the condition in which American foreign policy is made. United States membership in the United Nations and other international organizations has added still another dimension to foreign affairs. Economic, social and humanitarian considerations must now influence policy to a degree never before experienced. The economic requirements of the developing nations, for instance, are of top priority and vital to their political stability. The frightening global population explosion and, as a consequence, the world crisis in food production are new problems which must be reckoned with if the United States, land of plenty, is to maintain friendly and mutually satisfying relations with the rest of the world. Lastly, the technological revolution in communications and the advent of the Nuclear and the Space Age have made international relations the single most important factor for the future of the world. The State Department has, therefore, an enormous task, and, to add to its burdens, the Department must also review all domestic policies of other government departments and agencies and must try to correlate all their activities which could affect our relations with nations abroad. To accomplish this complex and vital task, the Secretary of State has an enormous department working both in Washington and all over the world. All our affairs abroad are handled through ambassadors, ministers, consuls and other members of the Foreign Service. They not only carry out our foreign policy, but they are also responsible for any Americans traveling abroad and for supporting American business interests overseas. The Secretary of State is responsible for the issuance of passports, that is, the right to travel outside the United States, to citizens of the United States. In Washington the many members of the State Department staff not only work on the formulation of foreign policy, but they are also responsible for handling all business with the representatives of foreign nations accredited to the government of the United States.

In recent years the increased responsibilities of the Department of State and the required attendance of the Secretary of State himself at many international conferences have caused the size of the staff to expand greatly. From the original two-room office manned by a Secretary of State and a few assistants in a building then next to the White House on Pennsylvania Avenue, the State Department is now housed in many large office buildings containing many thousands of employees. The Secretary of State is now assisted by the Undersecretary, an Undersecretary for Economic or Political Affairs, depending upon the individual who holds the office, two Deputy Undersecretaries, one for Administration and the other for Political Affairs, twelve Assistant Secretaries, the Legal Adviser, and the Counselor and Chairman of the Policy Planning Staff. Each of these officials, needless to say, has many more assistants who carry out the work of the department. In recent years three other agencies have been created by Congress, two of which are directly within the jurisdiction of the State Department, the Agency for International Development and the Peace Corps. The heads of these agencies work closely with and report to the Secretary. The third, the Agency for Arms Control and Disarmament, is a separate agency, but it is housed in the Department of State and the Director is at all times closely associated with the Secretary. When the Secretary is abroad, these responsible top officials make it possible for foreign affairs to continue in his absence without a break. In the early days of our history there were only a few diplomatic missions abroad. There are now one hundred and twelve United States Embassies, two legations and over one hundred and seventy Consulates throughout the world. In addition, there are also ten Special United States' Missions to international organizations such as the United Nations, the International Atomic Energy Commission and the Organization of American States. There are few spots on earth in which the United States is not represented by a member of the Foreign Service or a special appointee of the President.

The complexity of the system of creating foreign policy is staggering and can only be handled by the division of work within the department. There is a bureau headed by an Assistant Secretary for each of the five areas into which the world is divided (Europe, the Near East and South Asia, East Asia and the Pacific, Inter-America, and Africa), and within each bureau are offices devoted entirely to the problems of the United States with regard to the countries within the geographical division. The United States' missions abroad send reports to Washington where the information in these reports is acted upon by all members of the department concerned with the particular country and often by the Secretary of State himself.

Working closely with the Secretary and top officials of the department is the Policy Planning Staff of the department. This committee, under the charimanship of the Counselor who ranks with the Assistant Secretary, studies the information received from abroad and proposes long range plans for American foreign policy which are passed along to the Secretary of State. He may then make a decision relating to a certain policy and advise the President. It is the President, however, who is always responsible for the final decision. His decision is what becomes official American foreign policy and is carried out by the State Department and the Foreign Service officers abroad.

If the Secretary of State had only to formulate foreign policy on the considerations of the reports of the Foreign Service alone, the job would be difficult enough. But, as has been stated above, on top of those considerations there are many other factors which exercise great influence on foreign policy. Congress, for instance, plays a very important role. Congress must appropriate all the money to pay for the conduct of foreign affairs. The opinions, therefore, of the Senators and Congressmen on foreign policy must be considered. Congressional relations are of such importance that an Assistant Secretary of State devotes all his time to Congress alone. Economics plays such a large role now in foreign policy that there is an Assistant Secretary responsible for all matters of an economic and financial nature. To make foreign policy effective requires an understanding public abroad and an intelligent citizenry at home. An Assistant Secretary of State for Public Affairs has therefore been added to the staff. His job is to develop policy regarding our information activities abroad and to keep the American people informed about our foreign policy, what it is and why it is so. He also keeps the Secretary of State informed as to the state of public opinion. Foreign affairs are so important to the American people that it is imperative that they understand what it is all about. Since 1961 when Congress passed the Mutual Educational and Cultural Exchange Act there has been another Assistant Secretary responsible for the Bureau of Educational and Cultural Affairs. This office supervises student and teacher exchange programs, foreign tours by American specialists, entertainment and sporting groups and promotes the establishment of chairs in American studies in foreign universities. It also directs American activities in the United Nations Educational, Social and Cultural Organization (UNESCO). This Bureau works closely with the United States Information Agency which, although an independent agency outside the State Department, carries out United States foreign policy by maintaining Information Centers and libraries abroad.

Another important division of the State Department is the Bureau of Security and Consular Affairs headed by an Administrator again equal in rank to an Assistant Secretary. This Bureau is better known than most to many millions of Americans because it administers the Passport Office. No one may travel abroad today without a passport issued by the government identifying the bearer as a citizen of the United States. The Visa Office within this Bureau issues permissions to foreigners who wish to come to the United States for a visit. Less known functions of the Bureau are its direction of the welfare and the protection of Americans abroad by the Office of Special Consular Services and its responsibility for coordinating and directing policies concerning displaced persons and refugees through the Office of Refugee and Migration. This latter function has evolved in answer to the tragic human problems resulting from the second World War and the ensuing Cold War.

The two new agencies which have recently been included

within the overall jurisdiction of the department reflect United States reaction to changing world conditions and problems. The Agency for International Development was created in 1961 to carry out the Foreign Assistance Act passed by Congress in that year. A.I.D. directs all nonmilitary United States foreign assistance programs around the world. These programs in general take the form of economic and technical aid through loans and by development grants to less developed nations. With American technical and financial assistance it is hoped that these nations will be able to build essential industries, develop modern farming techniques and promote health and educational facilities with which to establish viable political, social and economic systems. The Alliance for Progress, a specialized tailored program for the economic advancement of Latin America, is also administered by this Agency.

The Peace Corps is perhaps the most revolutionary program created by the United States since 1789. The law which established the Corps in 1961 stated that the purpose was "to promote world peace and friendship through a Peace Corps, which shall make available to interested countries and areas men and women of the United States qualified for service abroad and willing to serve, under conditions of hardship if necessary, to help the peoples of such countries and areas meeting their needs for trained manpower, and to help promote a better understanding of the American people on the part of the peoples served and a better understanding of other peoples on the part of the American people." Volunteers for the Peace Corps, who at the present time number in the thousands, are carefully chosen and trained for a period of months either by private agencies or on college campuses and then serve abroad for two years. Many upon their return have joined the National Teacher Training Corps, a program growing from the war on poverty, and have used their skills acquired in the less developed nations to combat the problems of their own society. Although there is practically no financial reward for a Peace Corps Volunteer, the satisfaction derived from the experience has proved to be almost universal and it is fair to say that this program has kindled the imagination of the American people and awakened in a large number the desire to serve the cause of international understanding and goodwill.

The Agency for Arms Control and Disarmament, although physically within the Department of State and in spite of the fact that its Director advises the Secretary of State, is structurally not part of the Department. It is an independent agency created by a 1961 Act of Congress and its primary responsibility, as its name suggests, is to control the spread of nuclear weapons and to work toward disarmament among the nations of the world to a degree compatible with national security. The creation of the agency reflects the growing dangers to the world of the nuclear potential. The aim of the United States is to work toward world peace, and the control of armaments is extremely necessary to the attainment of that goal. Much of the work of the officers of this agency takes place in New York at the United Nations and in Geneva, Switzerland, where for a period of years the United States and the Soviet Union principally have been trying to hammer out a mutually acceptable limitation of armaments. To date, the major accomplishment of the Agency was the Treaty which banned the testing of nuclear weapons in the atmosphere.

The running of such a tremendous organization as the State Department is an important job in itself. One of the Deputy Undersecretaries is responsible for the administration alone of the department. The Foreign Service and the employees of the department are under him, and it is his job to see that they work smoothly and efficiently. Another important task required of the State Department is to deal with all the foreign representatives in Washington. The Chief of Protocol is responsible for seeing that at all times correct, courteous procedure is followed in the relations with foreigners. An oversight or a discourtesy could cause an international incident, and the job of the Protocol Chief is not always an easy one.

Over all this complex and important department is the Secretary of State. He has one of the most difficult jobs in the United States government. In the complicated and turbulent world of today the foreign affairs of the United States are of vital importance to the security of the United States and to the whole of the free world. The Secretary of State has the responsibility of trying to formulate a safe and effective policy that will enhance the security and influence of the United States. In his role of adviser to the President, he becomes identified with all American actions abroad, and his job is often a thankless one. He is appointed by the President and holds his office only as long as the President wishes him to. If the President should disagree with his Secretary, the Secretary is obliged to conform or to tender his resignation. As the job of Secretary of State is purely political, when an Administration changes and the other party taken over the presidency, the Secretary of State and the undersecretary and many of the other high officials of the department are replaced. Many of the key ambassadors are also replaced, as they are often not career diplomats, but appointed for political reasons by the President. Were it not for the fact that beneath the political appointee level there are large numbers of nonpolitical, career Foreign Service officers, considerable chaos would occur each time an Administration ended. Although most of the top officials are usually replaced, the day-to-day work that goes into the conduct of foreign relations continues, and the incoming Secretary of State finds a competent and loyal staff with which to begin the monumental task of advising the President of the United States on foreign policy.

THE UNITED STATES TREASURY

Along with the Department of State at the beginning of the history of the United States under the Constitution in 1789, the Department of the Treasury was established. Originally, the Treasury Department was responsible simply for the management of all the nation's finances. As the years passed, however, and the nation grew, the Treasury has come to be responsible for many varied organizations all in some way or another related to the financial life of the United States. In organization and purpose, therefore, the Treasury differs from the Department of State. Whereas the State Department has the single purpose of making and carrying out foreign policy with its entire organization devoted to that function, the Treasury Department has many different functions, and its organization is more a confederation of different offices all under the direction of the Secretary of the Treasury. Today the department has under it the Office of the Comptroller of the Currency, the Bureau of Engraving and Printing, the Fiscal Service, the United States Savings Bond Division, the United States Mint, the Bureau of Internal Revenue, the Bureau of Customs and the Secret Service. Each of these groups has its own head, but each is subordinate to the Secretary of the Treasury.

In his role as manager of the country's finances, the Secretary of the Treasury has many responsibilities. He is the President's chief financial adviser and an important member of the Cabinet. Like the Secretary of State, he is appointed by the President and must be confirmed by the Senate. He, too, is a political figure and holds office only as long as the President does or for as long as the President wants him to. His job requires that he make policies designed to improve the management of the nation's revenue. He also keeps all the public accounts and au-

thorizes all the money that is issued from the Treasury to pay
the nation's debts. Should Congress request any information
relevant to his financial responsibilities, the Secretary is obliged
to comply. Also each year he is required to present a report to
Congress on the financial state of the nation. Not only does the
Secretary perform all these duties, but he is also on many other
government and non-government boards, commissions and
councils. To name a few, he is the honorary Treasurer of the
American Red Cross, the Chairman of the Library of Congress
Trust Fund Board, the Chairman of the National Advisory
Council on International Monetary and Financial Problems,
and the United States Governor of the International Bank and
Monetary Fund. To name all of his many board memberships

75

would require a page. Suffice it to say that his presence is required on the many different groups in Washington whose business relates to the government's finances in some way.

To help him with these varied responsibilities, the Secretary has two Undersecretaries, nine Assistant Secretaries, a General Counsel, a Special Assistant for Law Enforcement, plus their assistants, as well as the heads of the departments under the Treasury. Again the size of the job has required the addition of many extra men to accomplish all the work of the Treasury. It is the Secretary alone, however, who is the President's chief adviser for financial policy, and his position as chief financial expert of the government makes his opinion weigh heavily among the Secretaries of the other departments.

Money is clearly the most important subject in the Treasury. It is not surprising then that several of the Treasury's subdivisions concern themselves exclusively with money, its creation and its use. The Office of the Comptroller of the Currency, the Fiscal Service, the Bureau of Engraving and Printing and the United States Mint all have to do directly with aspects of the nation's complicated financial life. One of the important changes made when the Constitution was adopted was the introduction of only one kind of currency, the United States currency. In 1792, in order to make that one legal currency, the United States Mint was established. From that time on all the coins in use in the country have been made by the Mint and by the Mint alone. The Mint also strikes all medals for the government to be presented for acts of valor in time of war or for meritorious service to the nation. The Mint is run by a Director in Washington, but he is assisted in his task by subordinates in six field offices in various parts of the United States. Beside his job of striking the coins of the United States, the Director also administers the federal regulations concerning the mining, issuing and the general use of gold and silver in the nation. The

Bureau of Engraving and Printing, also administered by a Director, makes all the paper currency for use in the United States. Beside this important job, the Bureau prints all other government paper documents, bonds, bills, Treasury checks, and revenue, customs, postage and savings stamps and all White House invitations. No currency or government document is legal other than that produced by these two important divisions of the Treasury.

Much that contributes to the nation's stable financial life has to do with banking. The Office of the Comptroller of the Currency, which was created in 1863, has to do entirely with the National Banks of the United States. The Comptroller of the Currency regulates all the National Banks. The establishment of a new one, an addition or a branch to an existing one, or the liquidation of such a bank can only be effected with the approval of the Comptroller. His office also regulates the investments and the accounts of the National Banks. Once a year the Comptroller examines the financial condition of each of the National Banks in the country. This important office under the Treasury is one which does much to guarantee a stable financial system for Americans.

Another important division of the United States Treasury is the Fiscal Service. In 1940 a reorganization of the Treasury created this service which directs many Treasury operations regarding revenue. An Assistant Secretary heads the service under the supervision of one of the Undersecretaries. This office oversees many aspects of the finances of the country. The Bureau of Accounts, the Bureau of Public Debts and the Office of the Treasurer of the United States are all parts of the Fiscal Service. In general, this service is the bookkeeping department of the Treasury. The Fiscal Secretary is required to prepare statements of the actual cash reserves of the country at various times, and it is the job of his division to keep the day-to-day financial records. It is the Fiscal Service that keeps track of the money that is made, invested or spent by the United States Treasury.

Also under the Treasury and directly responsible to the Secretary are other divisions whose jobs are concerned with the collecting of United States revenue and the enforcement of laws regulating that collection. Their functions in those respects make it logical that they should be under the Treasury. The Bureau of Internal Revenue, the Department of United States Savings Bonds, the Bureau of Customs and the Secret Service make up the divisions of this nature.

Of all the revenue collection agencies perhaps none is as well known as the Bureau of Internal Revenue. This Bureau is headed by a Commissioner appointed by the President and confirmed by the Senate. His job is to see that all taxes providing for internal revenue are duly collected all over the United States. The Commissioner is in Washington, but his Bureau is decentralized and divided into seven geographical areas. It is to these field offices, each headed by a regional Commissioner, that all the taxes in the United States are paid. The Washington office of the Bureau is the national office which makes policy and provides overall direction for the regional offices. Aside from the collection of income taxes and other direct taxes, the Internal Revenue Bureau is also responsible for administering and enforcing the tax laws relating to alcoholic beverages, tobacco and guns.

The Internal Revenue Bureau provides all the tax forms for citizens to fill out and also provides free assistance for those who find the blanks confusing. Paying taxes is never pleasant, but the Internal Revenue Bureau tries to make it as easy as possible. To those who try to avoid their responsibilities, however, the Bureau is not lenient. Tax forms are processed very carefully. This auditing used to be handled individually by the many employees of the Service, but increasingly in recent years the returns are subjected to the infallible, impersonal scrutiny of the computer. This modern marvel has speeded up the auditing process and has resulted in far more accurate tax returns. When delinquents are discovered, the Bureau immediately goes into action. If the tax is to be paid, it is then promptly collected. In certain cases the Bureau takes criminal action in order to collect the tax that is owed to the government. On the other hand, this careful auditing has another purpose. Occasionally too much tax is paid. In that case, the surplus is refunded to the taxpayer. The job of collecting taxes from the many million citizens in the United States is gigantic, but it is carried out smoothly and efficiently by the Bureau of Internal Revenue.

The United States Savings Bonds Division is also a section of the Treasury that adds to the revenue of the nation, but in a way different from Internal Revenue. Whereas everyone in the United States is obligated by law to pay taxes, only those who wish do business with the Savings Bonds Division. The government offers for sale several kinds of bonds and savings stamps. In return for cash, the purchaser receives a bond. In a given number of years the purchaser can cash it in and then receives his full purchase price plus an extra sum of money in interest. The sale of United States Savings Bonds adds to the revenue of the country. The savings bond system that is presently in use was originally designed during the second World War, but its success was so great that it has been continued in the postwar years.

Anyone entering the United States from abroad by boat, airplane or car has reason to know about the United States Customs Bureau, a subdivision of the Treasury Department. Even before landing or docking a person returning from a trip must make out a statement declaring what articles he is bringing in with him to the United States from abroad. Everyone on a trip is allowed to bring in a certain amount of foreign goods duty free, but anything over that amount must be taxed. This law is for the protection of American merchandise. The declaration of goods is presented to the Customs Inspectors immediately upon entering the United States. They check the statement and then open and look through all the luggage to see that no contraband items are being smuggled in. Although this procedure may be a nuisance to the individual, it is an important and necessary precaution. Not only do the laws of the country demand that duty be paid on the importation of foreign goods over a certain amount, but they also forbid the smuggling in of many harmful items such as narcotics. The Customs officials, therefore, act not only as tax collectors, but also as law enforcement and detection agents, working closely with the Bureau of Narcotics and Dangerous Drugs in the Department of Justice.

The Customs officers do more than inspect luggage and collect duties from those who enter the country legitimately. In the execution of their job they are also called upon to patrol the borders of the United States to prevent smuggling from either Canada or Mexico. Officers on duty along the frontiers have the authority to apprehend any smuggler they find. This patrol duty can often be dangerous work. As they are the officers of the government on constant duty not only at the ports of entry, but also along the long and often lonely borders of the country, the Customs men handle a good deal of work for the State Department, the Atomic Energy Commission and the Maritime Administration. For the State Department they check visas and passports of Americans traveling to certain foreign countries. For the Atomic Energy Commission they check exports to prevent taking out of the country controlled materials of all kinds without the proper permit or license. For the Maritime Administration the Customs officers board the merchant ships as they enter ports all over the United States and, aside from checking for customs duties, they also check, of all things, the boilers in the engine rooms to detect causes of possible explosions. This particular duty had its origin many years ago in the early days of the steamboat. Then explosions were more common, and it was important to check boilers before a ship sailed or during its time at dock for the protection of the sailors and dockworkers. Also, for the Maritime Administration the Customs Bureau handles many other things: the registering of ships, the collection of tonnage duties, the recording of sales of vessels and the regulation of ships in the coasting and fishing trades, to name a few.

The Customs office seems to have varied duties. Essentially its purpose is to collect duties on imports and exports for the Treasury. That main job makes its location in the Treasury reasonable because the duties collected are part of the revenue of the United States. The subsidiary duties of the Customs officers all stem from the fact that they are the men who are on the scene at all times. If each task required a different individual to carry it out, the numbers of employees at each port of entry would be staggering. To handle the tasks efficiently and economically, the Customs Bureau takes over these additional duties for the several government offices concerned. This many dutied subdivision of the Treasury is headed by a Commissioner of Customs. The central office is in Washington, and there the Commissioner administers all the laws pertaining to the importing and taxing of foreign goods for the Secretary of the Treasury. The main body of the Bureau is, however, all along the boundaries of the country and in all the seaports and airports where twenty-four hours a day Customs officers maintain a watch for the Treasury.

The remaining division, the Secret Service, is under the Department of the Treasury because its job entails the enforcement of the laws of the country concerning the collection of revenue and the use of the legal currency. To make sure that only the Mint and the Bureau of Engraving and Printing issue the United States currency and to protect Americans from counterfeiters, the Secret Service was established in 1860. This division keeps a close watch for the counterfeiting of currency and all government printed documents, such as bonds, checks and the like. Should counterfeit bills be discovered, the Secret Service goes immediately after the criminals and apprehends them in the name of the United States government as counterfeiting is a federal offense. Over the years, however, the Secret Service's job has been expanded, and today it is responsible for the physical safety of the President of the United States and that of his family. They also must provide protection for the Vice-President should he request it. Former Presidents and widows of Presidents are also entitled to Secret Service protection for themselves and their families if they desire it. The Secret Service guards the President at all hours day and night. At times this can be a very dangerous job as in 1950 when assassins attempted to take the life of President Truman at Blair House. One of the officers of the Secret Service lost his life in the gun fight which ensued while saving the life of the President. The assassination of President Kennedy occurred despite the vigilance of the men assigned to protect him.

THE DEPARTMENT OF DEFENSE

Perhaps the single most important reason that the American form of government has worked so well over the years is its flexibility and ability to adapt to changing circumstances. The best proof of that statement is to be found in the history of the Department of Defense. The Department of Defense was established in 1949. Scientific achievements and developments in the field of weapons have outdated the standard, accepted ways of defending the country, and new methods and systems have had to be devised for the best protection of the nation in the atomic age.

Originally, the defense of the United States was the responsibility of a War Department and a Navy Department. George Washington established the War Department immediately following his first election, and the Navy Department, which includes the United States Marine Corps, was founded in 1798. These departments were run by Secretaries who were always civilians. The professional military men worked with the civilians, but were always subordinate to them. The Constitution set up a civilian government with the President of the country the Commander in Chief of the armed services, and in the service departments civilian control has always been essential.

Until the twentieth century these two separate departments were solely responsible for the defense of the United States. The invention and development of the airplane was the first event to cause changes in the military setup. When the airplane was adapted to military use, the Army built up its own air corps as did the Navy and the Marines. World War II so emphasized the importance of air in defense that following the war it became apparent that it should be a separate service. Thus the Air Force was established on equal status with the Navy and the Army.

Modern warfare has become so complex and the need for central defense policies so compelling that shortly after World War II Congress had to give consideration to the idea of abolishing the separate service departments and establishing a central defense organization in their place. In 1947 a step was taken in this direction, and the National Security Act created the National Military Establishment. In 1949, subsequent to amendments to the 1947 Act, the Defense Department was initially established, headed by a Secretary of Defense. Under him were

the Secretaries of the Army, Navy and the Air Force who, although they had lost their Cabinet seats, were still responsible for the separate administration of the three services.

In 1952 and again in 1958 primarily because of the advent of the Space Age with its rockets, guided missiles and satellites further reorganization was necessary. Experience had also proved that the 1949 Act did not give the Secretary sufficient

85

authority to run the department efficiently. Although the National Security Act and its amendments had ostensibly established one department for all defense, it actually had only superimposed a new office consisting of the Secretary of Defense, the Undersecretary and the Assistant Secretaries over and above the Secretaries of the Departments of the Army, the Navy and the Air Force. The Act had made the Secretary of Defense the President's chief adviser on military and defense policies, but it did not, however, grant him unquestioned authority over the three service departments to carry out efficiently his role as coordinator and overall director of the Defense Department. Specific restrictions on his authority seriously weakened his position. The Act, for instance, expressly forbade the Secretary of Defense any transferring, reassigning, abolishing or consolidating of combatant and other functions assigned to the services. The Secretary was only to formulate policy and had not the undisputed authority to carry it out if the service Secretaries disagreed with him. His authority could also be challenged by the fact that the three service Secretaries could, if they felt strongly enough, bypass the Secretary of Defense, although a member of the Cabinet, and go directly to the President or to Congress. The Secretary's role was also made difficult because the services had been traditionally separate, and a keen rivalry marked their relations from the West Point-Annapolis football level straight up to the top commanding officers.

The Secretaries of the Army and the Navy Departments had been the civilian heads of the services for well over a hundred years. It was not surprising that this first reorganization of the defense setup only took the first steps toward the unification of the services and left much of the old pattern unchanged. Therefore, to make the Department more efficient and to clarify the position of the Secretary, Congress in 1958 passed the Department of Defense Reorganization Act. By this Act the Secretary was given the authority to coordinate the military departments of the Army, the Navy (including the United States Marine Corps) and the Air Force, thereby eliminating unnecessary duplication and providing more economical administration of the nation's defense. The Act, however, specifically forbids the merger of the services and each branch of the military is still headed by a Secretary and is organized independently of the others.

The present Department of Defense, housed in the famous Pentagon Building in Washington, consists of the Secretary of Defense, his Deputy, Assistant Secretaries, the Defense Staff Offices, the Joint Staff and the three military departments, each with its own Secretary, assistants and the men of the armed forces. The Secretary of Defense himself is the President's chief adviser on all defense matters and the Deputy is responsible for supervising and coordinating all activities of the department. Both positions as well as the Secretaries and Assistant Secretaries of the military services must be held by civilians appointed by the President and confirmed by the Senate. Thus the constitutional provision that the military be subordinate to the civilian is carried out. The professional military, however, is essential to the formulation of defense policy and to its being effectively implemented. The principal military advisers to the President, to the Secretary of Defense and to the National Security Council are the Joint Chiefs of Staff. This Staff is appointed by the President and confirmed by the Senate and consists of the Chairman and the Chief of Staff, United States Army, the Chief of Naval Operations, the Chief of Staff, United States Air Force and the Commandant of the Marine Corps. The latter, although he sits regularly with the others, only enters discussion as a co-equal when Marine Corps affairs are under review. The Joint Chiefs are the senior military com-

manders of the United States Defense establishment and they are the vital link in the chain of command that goes from the President to the Secretary of Defense to the commanders of each of the armed services.

In addition to the actual military and civilian leaders the Pentagon also houses many other departments each related to the nation's defense. One of the most interesting is the Office of Research and Engineering. Under the guidance of its Director who reports directly to the Secretary, this office is charged with conducting research into all sorts of new fields and evaluating the results as to their usefulness to the defense of the United States. Although most of the research has to do with weaponry, one particular piece of research led not only to the saving of a great deal of money but also to the boosting of the morale of the American fighting forces in Vietnam. Lettuce is a particularly perishable item and until recently was virtually denied to the soldiers in Southeast Asia because it cost a great deal to ship across the Pacific Ocean and the rate of spoilage was too high. Through the Office of Research and Engineering a method was found by which lettuce could be dehydrated and therefore shipped in bulk by air without spoilage and then reconstituted upon arrival. The United States servicemen, hungry for fresh salad, are now eating this lettuce regularly.

Another recent addition to the Pentagon Staff which reflects modern developments and techniques is the Assistant Secretary for Systems Analysis. His office has the responsibility of determining for the Secretary the cost effectiveness of all defense requirements, weapon systems, materiel and manpower. The creation of this office indicates the importance of relating the price of an effective defense system to the overall economy of the nation in today's world in which the cost of modern weapons and defense systems are unbelievably high.

The Department of Defense is without doubt the most complicated within the Executive branch of the government bearing a heavy burden of responsibility for the effective defense of a nation of almost two hundred million people. Its charter as prescribed by law is deceptively simple. The Defense Department's mission is "to support and defend the Constitution of the United States against all enemies, foreign and domestic, to insure, by timely and effective military action, the security of the United States, its possessions, and areas vital to its interest, to uphold and advance the national policies and interest of the United States and to safeguard the internal security of the United States." To implement these responsibilities is the task of the Secretary, his assistants and the commanders of the Armed Forces. In this Atomic and Space Age they have with the exception of the President the most difficult and vital job in the United States government.

THE DEPARTMENT OF JUSTICE

The Department of Justice is the legal branch of the United States government. Under its direction are many bureaus and divisions each concerned with one part of the many sided job of enforcing the federal laws and the carrying out of justice in the nation. Justice, like many of the Executive departments, has grown tremendously since its establishment.

In 1789, to enforce the federal laws and to advise the President on legal matters, the Congress created the post of Attorney General of the United States. At that time the Attorney General had no department under him. He simply advised the President and carried out the federal laws with the help of a few assistants. In 1870 the need for a department organized to meet the growing demands of insuring justice became obvious, and in that year the Department of Justice was established by Act of Congress. The Attorney General heads the department and is the Secretary of Justice, despite his different title.

The Department of Justice has, in general, five major jobs to perform. It is the federal law enforcement agency. It supplies the lawyers who represent the United States government in all cases to which it is a party in the federal courts. It runs all the federal prisons, and it is responsible for the discovery of violations of federal laws and the investigation of those violations. Lastly, the Attorney General with the help of his subordinates is the President's adviser on all legal problems confronting the Executive branch. The department also gives legal aid to any of the other Executive offices if it is requested. To carry out these many jobs, the Department of Justice is organized into subdivisions, each entrusted with one of the aspects of maintaining justice in the nation.

The Attorney General primarily is concerned with advising

the President and only in cases of exceptional seriousness does he argue the government's case in the Supreme Court. Under him is the Deputy Attorney General whose main function is to run the department and to be the chief liaison officer for Congress and the other Executive departments. The man whose job it is to represent the United States in the Supreme Court except in cases where the Attorney General himself argues is the Solicitor General. For a lawyer this is one of the most fascinating jobs in the government. The Solicitor General also has the sole authority to send any United States case to an appellate court. Much of the work of the department is carried out by another important assistant to the Attorney General, the Legal Counsel. He, with the help of his staff, prepares all the formal opinions of the Attorney General and assists him with his Cabinet responsibilities. The Counsel must also review the legality of all the Executive orders and proclamations. Should any gift or bequest, a gift made in a will, be made to the federal government, the Legal Counsel must decide whether it is legal or not for the government to accept it. His office also deals with any cases concerning conscientious objectors arising under any of the Military Service Acts of Congress. Another assistant to the Attorney General is the Pardon Attorney. All requests to the President for clemency are reviewed by his office, and recommendations are made by the Pardon Attorney to the Attorney General for the President's consideration. The President, however, takes the responsibility of making the final decision in these cases.

Since the establishment of the United States the number of subjects covered by federal statutes has steadily increased. As the Department of Justice is responsible for providing the means for enforcing all federal laws, it must have sufficient personnel and an efficient organization to carry out this task. Each subject covered by federal law, such as taxes, antitrust and internal security, to name a few, is the exclusive responsibility of a division within the department. Each division is headed by an Assistant Attorney General and is manned by lawyers who specialize in the kind of law related to their division. These attorneys actually bring the lawsuits in the name of the United States against violators of federal statutes. They prepare the briefs and argue the cases before federal judges.

It is important to note that these lawyers are in no position of favor before the Bench just because they represent the federal government. If they cannot prove their case to the Court, they lose. When a Justice Department lawyer loses a case, the case can be appealed if the Solicitor General in consultation with the division's attorneys decides to do so.

These divisions within the Justice Department often work closely with other government departments and agencies. The Anti-Trust division's work, for instance, is allied with that of the Federal Trade Commission. The Anti-Trust division's responsibility is to prevent monopolistic practices in businesses as defined by the Sherman Act of 1890. The Federal Trade Commission protects the public against monopolistic practices as defined by the Clayton Act, the Federal Trade Commission Act and various other Acts. The broad provisions of the Sherman Act often results in an overlapping of responsibility between the two groups. Rather than resulting in confusion, however, this occasional paralleling of responsibility results in better safeguards against illegal monopolies or restraints of trade. The number of cases is unfortunately sufficiently large to keep both offices busy and to prevent any serious conflicts of jurisdiction. The two offices work together toward the same end, to protect the public from illegal trust practices.

One of the most important aspects of the task of carrying out the laws of the country is the detection of violations of those laws. Before the lawyers of the Department of Justice can put the machinery of justice into motion, crimes must be discovered. The Federal Bureau of Investigation is the division of the department responsible for the detection of all violations of federal statute. The F.B.I. is one of the best known of all the government operations. It is essentially a large detective agency, and its activities cover all violations of federal laws except those specifically assigned to other departments. Counterfeiting, for example, is the responsibility of the Secret Service division of the Treasury Department. The job of the Federal Bureau of Investigation is a big one. Its specially trained agents protect Americans against the crimes of espionage, sabotage, treason and kidnapping, to name but a few.

As the name suggests, the F.B.I. only enters cases when a federal law has been violated. Crimes committed within State borders are the responsibility of local authorities, except those of espionage and sabotage which are always the responsibility of the federal bureau. To accomplish their task, the F.B.I. has agents all over the United States who operate out of field or branch offices. The central office in Washington administers the entire organization, keeps the criminal files and does all the laboratory work connected with crime detection. All the latest modern devices are used, and the speed with which the F.B.I. can work is one of the best safeguards of Americans against widespread crime. The record of the Bureau is a good one, and it rarely fails to solve a case. During the war, particularly, the work of the F.B.I. agents in detecting and foiling espionage and sabotage plots was impressive.

The Federal Bureau of Investigation's reputation for efficiency has done much to deter crime in the United States. Proof of this statement can be found in the decline in the number of kidnapping cases. Until the "gangster era" of the 1920's and early 1930's kidnapping was not a common crime, and there were no federal laws concerning it. In the early thirties, however, kidnapping suddenly became a crime of national proportions. Criminals found it a profitable business. Horrible as this was, it was not until the brutal murder of the kidnapped Lindbergh baby that the nation's conscience was aroused to such an extent that Congress enacted a law in 1932 making kidnapping a federal crime with the death penalty as punishment. The apprehension of the guilty party by the F.B.I. in the famous case, and his subsequent electrocution after trial did much to end this frightful criminal activity. Though there are still those who think they can break the law and get away with it, the swift efficiency of the F.B.I. has reduced the incident of serious crime greatly in the nation since the "gangster era," and its agents well deserve their fame.

Another major division of the Department of Justice is the Bureau of Immigration and Naturalization. This bureau, originally established in 1891, used to be in the Department of Labor, but in 1940 it was transferred to Justice. The history of this bureau is of particular interest in that it reflects a fundamental change in American policy. Until the late nineteenth century there were no immigration laws in the United States. As everyone knows, the country was populated from the beginning by immigrants who came to seek a new life in a new land. In the early days of our country there was little need for any restrictions on immigration. There was plenty of land and many jobs for all comers. As the western frontiers were pushed back and the population increased, however, it occurred to some that, if unrestricted immigration continued indefinitely, the country would become overpopulated and the means of making a living would become hazardous. That point of view led to the passage of laws designed to regulate and limit the immigration into the United States from other nations of the world. Basically immigration laws are for the protection of the American citizens and their jobs. Since much of immigration affected the labor supply in this country, it was logical to place the first Immigration Bureau in the Department of Labor. Changing world conditions and the emergence of different political philosophies in the mid-twentieth century have led to a change in the nature of American immigration policy. In the World War II decade it was not only a question of how many new citizens could the United States absorb, but also, and most importantly, a question of what kind of immigrant and what ideas did he hold. With the world in a state of uneasy division between the free and the Communist countries the United States looked at each immigrant more carefully. No one who did not believe wholeheartedly in democracy was welcome. For these reasons the Bureau of Immigration and Naturalization was moved to the Department of Justice which is responsible for the internal security of the nation. Its officers, however, still work closely with the Department of Labor because in the 1960's United States immigration policy was broadened to include not only those who had relatives in the United States but also those who possess skills needed by this country.

The Immigration division of Justice administers the immigration and naturalization laws. Its officers are responsible for the admission of aliens, non-Americans, and their exclusion should they be discovered to be undesirable. Agents of the Bureau also patrol the borders of the nation to prevent illegal entry of immigrants. In this respect they work with the Coast Guard which patrols the oceans and the Customs Bureau which also patrols the frontiers.

For those immigrants who enter the country legally, the Bureau also supervises the naturalization laws. Each immigrant who wants the privileges and protections of an American citizen must be naturalized. After five years of residence in the United States the alien must pass a test to prove his knowledge of the American form of government and must swear allegience to the United States, forsaking all affiliation to any foreign country. The naturalization of immigrants is an important step, and it is recognized as such. Federal courts as well as some State courts all over the United States hold the naturalization ceremonies, and the swearing in of new citizens is an impressive experience. Even though unrestricted immigration is no longer possible, the naturalization ceremony is a reminder of the fact that the United States was created by immigrants and has always been a haven for those wishing to seek a better life in freedom.

As has been mentioned, the United States government is constantly being reorganized so that it can meet the challenges of new problems which arise as times change. In recent years the Department of Justice has been given additional responsibilities to enable the federal government to deal more effectively with two serious problems which have exploded on the national scene in the 1960's, the problem of insuring civil rights to every American and the equally serious problem of controlling the use of narcotics.

In 1957 a new Division of Civil Rights headed by an Assistant Attorney General was created within the Department of Justice. As Congress has extended the authority of the federal government over the area of civil rights, so has the responsibility of this Assistant Attorney General been broadened. He and his division are directly charged with the enforcement of all the civil rights laws—the right to vote, the right to trial with an impartial jury, the right to education without discrimination, the right to use all public accommodations freely, the right to fair practices of employment and the right to open housing. The Civil Rights Division investigates all complaints by citizens who claim they have been denied their rights. In the case of voting rights, federal examiners are appointed to oversee local elections to guarantee that all who vote under law are, in fact, able to register and cast their ballot. The Assistant Attorney General in charge of this division also has the authority to initiate suits in federal courts in cases where civil rights have been abused. Not all of his job, however, is involved with policing. His division also works through Community Relations Service which was moved recently from the Department of Commerce to the Department of Justice. This service seeks to erase problems of racial origin before they erupt and, therefore, require legal action. The officers assigned to this division work with communities across the land through the communications media helping them to identify sources of racial friction and to understand the civil rights laws. Theirs is a positive approach to the correcting of the wrongs of society and to creating an America in which all citizens in fact enjoy their constitutional privileges, and because of their work it is hoped that the Division of Civil Rights will in the course of time find that it has fewer and fewer cases to prosecute.

As the problem of civil rights has become acute in recent years requiring a realignment of federal authority, so has the equally urgent problem of narcotics required similar reorganization of the federal government's control. For many years there were two divisions within the federal government charged with authority over narcotics and drug control. One was the Bureau of Narcotics in the Treasury and the other was the Bureau of Drug Abuse Control in the Department of Health, Education and Welfare. In 1968 these two Bureaus were moved into the Department of Justice where they have been combined in the Bureau of Narcotics and Dangerous Drugs. The Bureau of Narcotics was originally in the Treasury because it had the responsibility of safeguarding the country against the abuse of the laws controlling the importing, growing and selling of narcotics. As much of the illicit traffic in drugs originated abroad, the Narcotics Bureau worked closely with the Bureau of Customs and the Coast Guard, both then in the Treasury. The Bureau of Drug Control Abuse, originally part of the Food and Drug Administration within the Department of Health, Education and Welfare, had the duty of accounting for and regulating the manufacture and sale of stimulant and depressant drugs within the United States as well as conducting programs to educate the populace as to the social, psychological and physiological effects of drug abuse. In recent years drug abuse has increased alarmingly, and Congress by combining the divisions and placing them in the Department of Justice has given the Bureau increased authority to control the problem. This Bureau, although not one of the best known in the government, is of great importance to the welfare of the American people. Narcotics are all the drugs such as marijuana, heroin, and opium which, though perfectly safe when used in medicines, are extremely dangerous when freely circulated. The uncontrolled use of narcotics leads to addiction which can result in either insanity or death. Because of their potentially dangerous and lethal qualities, the importation and use of narcotics are strictly regulated by federal law for the protection of the nation. It is the sole job of the Bureau of Narcotics and Dangerous Drugs to see that the laws applying to narcotics are obeyed. The Bureau regulates the narcotics trade by issuing licenses to those legally permitted to use the drugs. The narcotics agents work closely with the United States Public Health Service in controlling the use of drugs within the country and with the International Police agency, Interpol, in controlling the manufacture, sale and distribution of drugs abroad. Within the United States when the agents find a violation of the federal laws, they act as a police force in apprehending the criminals, and their co-workers in Justice then prosecute the case. Unfortunately, the traffic in illegal drugs is an extremely profitable one and there are all too many attempts to circumvent the law.

The Bureau of Narcotics and Dangerous Drugs not only has a full-time job, but one of vital concern to all Americans who are aware of the tragedy of drug addiction.

POST OFFICE DEPARTMENT

Consider what it would be like to have no mail. It would be unthinkable. Every American takes for granted that no matter what the situation or the weather the mail will be delivered. Nothing is more common in an American's life than the corner postbox or the familiar figure in blue-gray carrying his sack. Communication has always been essential, and, in the days before the telegraph, telephone and radio, mail was the only means of communication between people who lived beyond speaking distance. It is not surprising, therefore, that the postal system in the United States dates back to colonial days. Before the Revolution the British had a well-organized postal system in the American colonies. None other than Benjamin Franklin was largely responsible for its operation. In 1737 he was first appointed Postmaster General of Philadelphia, and in 1757 he became the Co-Deputy Postmaster General for all the British colonies. After the outbreak of the Revolution in 1775 the Continental Congress appointed him the first American Postmaster General. Much of the organization of the present postal system is due to his wise and practical methods in the days of the rebelling colonies.

The importance of a postal system was so great that even under the Articles of Confederation in 1777 the otherwise feeble Congress had the sole authority in the new nation to establish post offices, post roads and to issue stamps in order to pay for their expenses. In 1789 after the adoption of the Constitution, Congress created the Office of Postmaster General. At that time, however, the Postmaster General had no department nor was he of Cabinet rank. Andrew Jackson in 1829 began the tra-dition that the Postmaster General should have a seat in the Cabinet by inviting the then incumbent to join it. Oddly enough, it was not until 1872, however, that Congress finally established the Post Office Department and that the Postmaster General became officially a member of the Cabinet by law. From then until the present the Post Office has been a regular Executive department, and today the Postmaster General actually runs the largest business in the entire United States.

Although originally the function of the Post Office was sim-ply to see to the delivery of the mail in the most efficient man-ner possible and to establish post roads over which the mail would be carried, in today's world the department has had to embrace many additional functions. Postage stamps of all de-nominations are issued by the Post Office, and many types of mail are now included in its service, such as rail and airmail, reg-istered mail, certified mail, collect-on-delivery service and par-cel post. All types of delivery, including city, rural-free-delivery and special delivery, are guaranteed by the depart-ment.

In the 1960's two new modes of operation have been introduced to enable the Post Office to deal with the enormous increase in the amount of mail it has to handle. The famous Zip Code has been devised to speed up mail delivery. Every city, town, county and hamlet in the United States is assigned a number and all articles of mail in order to reach their destina-tions promptly must bear the correct number. Big cities are as-signed one primary code number, 100 in the case of New York, and then in addition two other digits to designate to the central Post Office which section of the city or of the nearby suburbs the letter or package must be delivered.

At the same time that the Zip Code was invented, automation was also being introduced to sort out the tremendous volume of mail in a speedy and efficient system. In many major

cities no human hand touches the mail until the Postman carrier himself, for whom no substitute has been found, starts on his rounds with his bag. Automation which always sounds as if the human element has been erased actually affects the people using the mails by forcing them to change traditional habits. Packages, for instance, in the past always had to be addressed on both sides. Today only one side can be addressed so that the machine which sorts out the packages will not be confused. As people are slow to change, almost every postal clerk now has to take time out to paste over one set of addresses.

Although the Post Office Department is trying heroically

to conquer the problems presented by the ever increasing amounts of mail, by requiring the Zip Code, by introducing automation, and by increasing the cost of postage, unfortunately the expenses involved in delivering the mail speedily and efficiently have soared and the federal government has sustained serious financial losses every year. The situation has become so serious that it has even been proposed that the federal government give up its traditional role as mail carrier and that the department be reorganized as a government corporation. At this writing, however, this idea is simply a proposal and Uncle Sam is still responsible for delivering the mail.

Beside the problem of carrying and delivering the mail, the Postal authority also includes certain law enforcement activities. The mails cannot be used for the transmittal of obscene literature; they may not be used for lotteries which are a form of gambling; they may not be used for fraudulent purposes; and they cannot be used for the shipping of liquor or inflammables. Postal inspectors have the responsibility of checking the mails and making sure that they are not being used illegally. Should any unlawful use be detected, the inspector who discovers it reports to the Chief Hearing Examiner of the Post Office. He acts as a trial examiner and makes initial decisions in these cases. If the case cannot be settled by the Examiner, the Department of Justice then takes over, and the case is decided in the federal courts.

The organization of the Post Office differs slightly from that of the other Executive departments. The President appoints the Postmaster General in whom by law rests all the authority of the department. He may, however, delegate authority to subordinates if he so wishes within the department. He has a Deputy who is also appointed by the President and who is fully responsible for the department's authority in the absence of the Postmaster General. All other assistants, the Legal Counsel and postmasters of the first, second and third class level are all appointed by the President on the recommendation of the Postmaster General. The officers who fall below this level are all appointed by the Postmaster General. To insure efficient mail service, the country is divided into regions at the head of which are Regional Directors. Under their supervision are all the Post Offices in the region, and they are responsible to the national Post Office Department for their administration. The Post Office Department, as has already been stated, is the largest business enterprise in the nation. Whereas there were seventy-five offices in 1789, today there are over thirty-seven thousand throughout the United States. Each not only collects mail and sees it off to its proper destination, but delivers all the incoming mail one or more times a day. To make this operation run as efficiently as it does is a mammoth job, and the duties of the Postmaster General, though perhaps not glamorous, are ones vital to the orderly functioning of the nation and personally important to each individual who looks forward to the mail.

THE DEPARTMENT OF THE INTERIOR

Of all the Executive departments the Department of the Interior has changed the most in its more than one hundred years of history. Established by Act of Congress in 1849, Interior was originally really the housekeeper for the United States government. All matters having to do with the interior of the nation were dealt with by this department. It became a center for many bureaus and offices unrelated to each other, but fitting under none of the other Executive departments. As the federal government grew and the creation of new departments and independent agencies was necessary, the nature of the Department of the Interior changed also. Today the department is primarily the custodian of the nation's natural resources. It still is, however, a department whose responsibilities cover seemingly unrelated offices. Although its main function is to make the most of the natural wealth of the country for better peacetime living and for unpreparedness in case of war, Interior still has some of its old responsibilities to look after also. Therefore, to understand the makeup of the department, it is best to divide its functions into three major fields, the administration of Indian affairs, the direction of all the United States territories and trusts abroad, and the custodianship of the nation's natural resources.

Between the adoption of the Constitution and 1824 no one in the government gave much thought to the problems of the American Indians. Ever since the days of the earliest settlers, the Indians had simply been displaced by the white men. They were pushed west each time a white settlement was founded. This pattern repeated itself from 1609 until the early nineteenth century. In 1803 Thomas Jefferson's purchase of the Louisiana territory from Napoleon added an enormous piece of land to the United States. In the years that followed a great western migration took place. By 1824 it was obvious that something had to be done about the original inhabitants of the land, the Indians. In that year the first Bureau of Indian Affairs was created and placed under the direction of the War Department. The army had much to do with protecting the white settlers in the early days of the West, and it was logical that Indian relations should be carried out by the military. In 1849, however, the Bureau of Indian Affairs was transferred to the newly created Department of the Interior. There the Bureau has remained.

The purpose of the Bureau is to act like a friendly uncle to the Indians. It supervises the many reservations on which the remaining tribes live. The aim of the Bureau is to help the Indians to adjust their social, economic and political lives to the conditions of the twentieth century. The officers of the Bureau assist the Indians to achieve independence and look forward to the day when the tribes can operate without government aid. Until the termination of government assistance is possible, the Bureau acts as a trustee for Indian lands and wealth, helping the owners to realize the most they can from their possessions. In the fields of health, welfare and education the Bureau is also very active, and individual Indians who wish to break away from tribal life are assisted by the Bureau to become productive American citizens. The energies of the Bureau are entirely directed toward educating and preparing the Indians for participation in the affairs of the United States and toward ending their second-class citizenship. Perhaps the conscience of the white men who displaced the Indian from his land so abruptly was pricked, and the establishment of the Bureau of Indian Affairs was an attempt to make up for so many years of neglect and maltreatment.

The Bureau of Indian Affairs is centered in Washington and its Director is responsible to the Secretary of the Interior. Most of its work, however, is accomplished in the fields where there are roughly sixty Indian projects across the nation. The Washington office serves in an administrative and policy making capacity. The Director is also responsible for asking Congress for the appropriation of money with which to run Indian Affairs.

Another subdivision of the work of the Interior Department is the section devoted to the territories and the trust areas of the United States abroad. The territories belonging to the United States now include the Virgin Islands, Guam and American Samoa. The former Japanese Mandates in the Pacific, the Marshall, Mariana and Caroline Islands, are still under United States trusteeship within the United Nations. Puerto Rico, a former territory, now has commonwealth status, and as it has its own agency, is no longer under the Department of the Interior.

Each of the United States territories has its own governor who is appointed by the President and must be confirmed by the Senate and each also elects every two years a nonvoting delegate to the United States House of Representatives. In general, the Office of Territories in the Department of the Interior assists the governors of each territory. The purpose of the office is to encourage social, economic and political development in the territories and to coordinate their affairs with the overall defense policies of the nation.

The trust territories under the Office of Territories are a post-World War II responsibility. Following the defeat of Japan, the United States took over the administration of the Japanese Mandates in the Pacific as part of its responsibility under the United Nations. The Office gives the High Commissioner of these islands any assistance that he requests.

The staff of the Office of Territories reports directly to the Secretary of the Interior and is responsible for keeping him informed as to the affairs of the areas so that he, in turn, may advise the President.

The third responsibility of the Department of the Interior is made up of many parts, all having something to do with the natural resources of the United States. The aim of Interior is to manage, conserve and develop every natural resource of the nation to the greatest possible degree. The natural wealth of the country includes so many things that to achieve the purpose there are as many offices and bureaus as there are natural resources. Lands, mines, oil, gas, water, reclamation, fish and wildlife . . . all the concern of an office or bureau in the Department of the Interior.

Each office or bureau helps the Secretary of the Interior in some way to improve the use of the natural wealth of the United States. Much of the work of the various offices has to do with research and information. Under the department's jurisdiction are some four hundred and fifty-six million acres of land owned by the federal government. This land is managed by the Bureau of Land Management for the benefit of the nation. The Bureau's activities relate to experimenting with conservation measures and the classification of types of land.

Water is probably one of the largest of all subjects studied by the Department of the Interior. Many offices share in the working out of better systems of using the water in the country. The Bureau of Reclamation works throughout the nation improving methods of irrigation and studying ways of controlling floods. Three separate Power Administrations; the Bonneville in Portland, Oregon; the Southeastern in Elberton, Georgia; and the Southwestern in Tulsa, Oklahoma; operate federal dams which generate electricity and encourage the greater use of this source of power by selling it at low rates. Thereby they improve the standard of living of the many Americans living in the regions covered by the three projects. The Office of Saline Water experiments with ways to transform sea water into usable fresh water, and other offices deal with the use of water for hydroelectric purposes and help with the administration of the federal dams in the country.

One of the newest and most important subdivisions dealing with water is the Federal Water Pollution Control Administration which was created by Congress in 1965 in response to the sudden awareness of the seriousness of the problem of the pollution of the nation's water resources. Unfortunately, in this case Congress may have acted too late to prevent a major disaster from overtaking the United States. For years industrial wastes and sewage have been pouring unchecked into the nation's harbors, rivers and lakes, polluting the water, killing the fish and the bird life, thereby seriously affecting the ecological balance. It was not until three major instances of water pollution and their consequences occurred, each widely publicized, that the federal government took action. There was a widespread epidemic of hepatitis along the eastern coast; there was the sudden killing of hundreds of thousands of fish in the Great Lakes; and there suddenly appeared foamy suds in many of the streams and rivers across the nation caused, it turned out, by detergents emptied into the waterways from dishpans and washing machines.

Congress, by passing the Water Quality Act in 1965 establishing the Federal Water Pollution Control Administration, attempted, perhaps vainly, not only to stem the speed at which pollution was ruining the water resources of the country, but to prevent further pollution from occurring. The mission of the Administration is to design special programs to eliminate pollution from the interstate waterways, to help States with awards of federal funds to conduct their own anti-pollution programs, to encourage the enactment of State anti-pollution laws, and to promote research into ways by which industrial waste and sewage can be disposed of without being dumped raw into waterways. Although more and more Americans are coming to support the federal efforts to stem the lethal tide of pollution, the government has a very hard time achieving its aim of making the nation's water supply pure again. It is extremely costly, for instance, for industry to dispose effectively of wastes scientifically. Also, the federal efforts are hampered by the fact that State governments constitutionally control intrastate affairs and in many cases water pollution within a State which is not affected by federal law spreads its contamination by seepage into interstate waterways which are under federal control. What really would help the federal government to succeed in controlling pollution is a massive educational campaign to make every single American aware of the vital need for pure water for the very survival of the nation.

Another major concern of bureaus within Interior is the conservation and use of the mineral resources under the land. Health and safety measures are worked out and put into practice to improve the working conditions of the nation's miners. The Interior Department also controls the fish and wildlife of the United States. The Fish and Wildlife Service works not only to preserve animals and birds, but also has the important job of working out international agreements in conjunction with the State Department relating to migratory birds and fish. All of these offices collect and study material about the natural resources of the country, and then it is made available to the public. This dissemination of valuable information helps the nation conserve and use its wealth to the best advantage.

One of the divisions of Interior that contributes a great deal to the American people in a pleasurable way is the National Parks Service. Anyone in the United States who has ever visited a National Park or an historical place of interest is aware of the work of this service. It not only is responsible for the creation and maintenance of the National Parks throughout the country, but also provides educational and historical information for anyone interested. Much of the nation's natural lore is explained by the well-trained staffs who run the parks. Also they have done a superb job in presenting American history in a clear and interesting fashion at the many battlefields and other places of historical importance in the United States.

Administering the enormous Department of the Interior is the Secretary of the Interior and his assistants. The Secretary himself is a member of the Cabinet, appointed by the President and confirmed by the Senate. His deputy is the Undersecretary, and he also has seven Assistant Secretaries and a Legal Adviser. Each of the Assistant Secretaries is responsible for one or more of the many offices within the department. All subordinates report to the Secretary whose primary task it is to inform and advise the President on the many subjects covered by the

Interior Department. Without this housekeeper and watchdog over the resources of this bountiful land, much that we as citizens take for granted would have been destroyed or wasted, and the nation would be immeasurably poorer for it.

THE DEPARTMENT OF AGRICULTURE

Agriculture is the most fundamental of men's activities. It is the science of growing crops and raising livestock. Without agriculture no human life could be sustained. In modern times agriculture has become more important than ever. Much of the population of the United States today lives in cities or in suburban areas, and, consequently, depends entirely on others, the farmers of the nation, to provide them with food and clothing. No longer can men supply themselves with their fundamental needs as they could in the past. As America grew, so did the need for a department of the federal government to concern itself solely with the problems of agriculture. The large Department of Agriculture today, though, hardly resembles the small office set up in 1862.

Congress in that year established an agricultural department headed by a Commissioner who was not even a member of the Cabinet. In 1889 it was enlarged and made the eighth of the Executive departments. In that year the Secretary of Agriculture officially joined the President's Cabinet. Its size has continued to increase over the years, and today it is a large department with many different responsibilities to carry out. The Secretary, appointed by the President and confirmed by the Senate, runs the department with the assistance of an Undersecretary and four Assistant Secretaries. As much of the department's work is with the States and with the individual farmers, there are offices scattered throughout the United States. Of all the departments of the federal government except perhaps the Post Office, the functions of Agriculture are the most closely associated with our daily lives.

The Department of Agriculture has many functions both national and international. One is purely concerned with scientific research for the improvement of the standards of living of the American people. All information collected from research is available to the public. Conservation of soil, forests and water is another concern, and a third is the carrying out of the federal laws relating to meat inspection. Marketing services for farmers here in the United States and the development of markets in foreign countries are other functions of the department. Lastly, the department administers all federal farm programs enacted by Congress.

The Agricultural Research Service is the section of the department responsible for the improvement of foods, crops, livestock, home economics and clothing. In Beltsville, Maryland, there is a twelve-thousand-acre agricultural center at which all crops, food and livestock research is conducted. Here soils are tested, fertilizers developed and new foods or types of foods experimented with. Two of the best known successes now available to Americans that were developed at Beltsville are the small turkey and zoysia grass designed to withstand everything including crabgrass. Not only does the research center find new and better ways of doing things, but it also combats animal diseases and plant pests. In this connection the division also administers all the laws relating to the quarantining of infected animals or plants or either of these imported into the United States from abroad. Beltsville is the largest of the research centers, but the Service works all over the country in cooperation with State experimental stations and often with private individuals. All the experimental stations in United States possessions abroad are also under the supervision of the Agricultural Research Service. In the Virgin Islands as well as in the Commonwealth of Puerto Rico, the Service is busily engaged in experimenting with ways of improving the standards of living of the inhabitants through agriculture.

Under the Research Service is also the Institute of Home Economics. This service, instituted in 1894, does research into nutrition, clothing, household economics and furnishings. The women of America have reason to be particularly grateful to this Institute. In every possible way it serves the homemaker. There is no question relating to the home and the family that cannot be answered by the service. Information concerning babies, furniture, diet and even domestic budgets is available to any interested person, and no problem is too small for the Institute. Even odd bugs that turn up in the home will be cheerfully identified, and the proper means of getting rid of them prescribed by this service.

The housewives of the nation are also protected by another branch of the Agricultural Research Service. All meat and poultry sold through interstate commerce in the United States must bear a stamp of inspection guaranteeing its wholesomeness and quality. Agents of this service operate all over the country not only inspecting meat for the tables of the nation, but also inspecting the abattoirs for cleanliness. Every consumer knows that her purchase is what the butcher says it is because of this careful inspection. Even dogs and cats are protected as the inspectors include in their duties the inspection of pet food. The nation's pets can be sure of good, healthy food in their bowls.

Conservation is a subject as important to the Department of Agriculture as it is to the Interior. The Agricultural Conservation Program Service runs the conservation activities for the department. In carrying out their responsibilities, the members work closely with the State Agricultural Departments and with the land-grant colleges. The land-grant colleges are colleges in the States and in the territories whose land was originally granted to the States by the federal government in order to provide institutions for the teaching of agricultural and mechanical knowledge. Today the federal government only contributes a small amount to the colleges, and the States manage them almost entirely. They are important, however, in the federal government's conservation programs. In cooperation with the State Agricultural Departments and the land-grant colleges the conservation programs of the federal government are carried out by means of a system of cost-sharing. The United States government shares the cost to the farmer or the rancher of the on-the-farm soil and water practices which are considered important for the conservation of these natural resources. This financial assistance to the individual farmers or ranchers results in greater conservation of cropland, pasture, ranges and forests, and naturally is a beneficial program for all Americans.

Separate, but closely allied to the conservation program are the Forest Service and the Soil Conservation Service of the Agriculture Department. The Forest Service maintains roughly one hundred and fifty national forests. The purposes of the Service are to protect trees from fire, insects of all kinds and diseases and to experiment with types of trees and to improve their economic uses. Many of the national forests serve as recreational spots for Americans to enjoy. The Soil Conservation Service concerns itself with helping the individual farmer plan his land in order to get the maximum productivity from it. The members of this service work in the field with the farmer personally and guide him through the various stages of scientific planning. Technical assistance is offered, and any special equipment needed to carry out the program may be obtained through the service. The farmer, however, does all the work. The service only advises.

The Agricultural Department is not merely concerned with the growing and the raising of better crops and animals, but also with the problems of the marketing of farm products and seeing that needy groups receive an adequate supply of food. One of its important services is that of the Marketing and Consumer Service. The function of this service is to make possible the widest and the most efficient distribution and marketing of farm goods for the whole Nation. Much of this work involves statistics, the putting together of facts which can be studied for the improvement of marketing all over the country. The staff also does much to try to foresee the outlook ahead for farm products and to predict markets to help the farmer in planning his crops. Under this Division are the inspection, classing and grading of crops for the protection of the consumers, and the administration of the federally supported school lunch, free milk programs and the Food Stamp Program. This program, established by Act of Congress in 1964, is part of the war on poverty. Needy families exchange the money they would normally spend for food for coupons of a higher monetary value. The coupons are then exchanged for food in stores participating in the program. The government then reimburses the merchants at the face value of the stamps. The work of the Marketing and Consumer Service is designed to help the farmer distribute his produce, to protect him from fraudulent marketing practices and through a variety of programs bring food to needy people to provide them with an adequate diet.

Much of our food is exported today, and it is the job of the Foreign Agricultural Service to represent the United States government in foreign agricultural matters. The office primarily develops markets abroad for United States products. Again much of the work involved is in collecting information and making it available to the American farmer. The service also arranges programs for visitors interested in American methods of agriculture, such as the group of Russian farmers who toured the United States a few years ago. In recent years the United States has concerned itself specifically with aiding developing countries in Asia, Africa and Latin America, and the Department of Agriculture has expanded its functions to include the management of the Food for Peace program inaugurated by Congress in 1966. The department procures agricultural products and exports them to the needy countries either as a donation to prevent famine or in return for services or foreign currencies. The Food for Peace program is one of the most important in proving to the less fortunate in the world the concern of the United States for human welfare. A land of plenty not only can but must share its bounty and by doing so the United States is making a significant contribution to peace.

The last major function of the Agricultural Department is to administer all federal laws pertaining to farm programs. Farming is a hazardous and uncertain occupation. The cost to the farmer of seed, fertilizer and machinery is great before he has a marketable product. Should any of nature's disasters, such as floods, droughts or pests befall him, he may be financially ruined. Also the price of farm goods is apt to fluctuate violently. A man may plant cotton, for instance, when the price is high, but by the time his cotton is ready for the market, the price may be way down. He is out of pocket. Many farmers who have experienced disasters of these kinds decided to give up and find more stable and secure ways of making a living. As agriculture is so necessary to an industrialized nation like ours, the government became concerned over the conditions of the farmers of America. Since the 1930's many various farm programs have been enacted by Congress in order to aid the farmer to make a decent living as well as to insure the production of enough of the agricultural goods upon which the life of the nation depends. It is the Department of Agriculture that carries out these programs through the Commodity Credit Corporation. Price supports, crop insurance and agricultural credit for farmers are some of the programs administered under the supervision of the department.

Most of the work of the Agriculture Department is carried out in the field rather than in Washington. In the capital, however, the Department of Agriculture offers many helpful services. One is the Office of Information which is responsible for the displays, photographs and movies in the Agriculture Department's building and for the collection of material for the press, radio and television. The National Agricultural Library contains books on every conceivable subject related to agriculture, and the public is welcome to use these sources of informa-

tion. The United States Department of Agriculture Graduate School is also in Washington. This school was established in 1921, and although it does not give a degree, its purpose is to improve the federal agricultural services by offering educational opportunities to federal employees. Interested students may either attend the school or enroll in the correspondence courses it offers. The school is run by a director and a general administrative board appointed by the Secretary of Agriculture and is a nonprofit organization.

THE DEPARTMENT OF COMMERCE

Commerce includes all business and trading activities. The Department of Commerce is the Executive department under the President responsible for all commercial affairs of the United States government. Its purpose is to encourage, promote and develop foreign and domestic commerce for the benefit of the citizens of the country. The present Department of Com-

117

merce was created by Act of Congress in 1913. Until that year there had been a Department of Commerce and Labor. The 1913 Act, however, separated the two and made each into a department headed by a Secretary of Cabinet rank.

The Department of Commerce is a confederation of many different offices and bureaus all in one way or another related to commerce, but often unrelated to each other. Over the whole department is the Secretary of Commerce who is appointed by the President and who must be confirmed by the Senate. His chief jobs are to supervise the department and to advise the President on all matters pertaining to the nation's commercial affairs. In his office and directly responsible to him is the Office of Public Information. This office collects and evaluates all kinds of commercial information and advises the Secretary. Also directly responsible to the Secretary is the department's General Counsel. He and his staff attend to all legal matters and handle all the department's relations with Congress. The Counsel also helps the Secretary in an advisory capacity.

Assisting the Secretary and in charge of the many and varied functions of the Department of Commerce are the Undersecretary and five Assistant Secretaries. In the 1960's the Department of Commerce was completely reorganized when its responsibilities in regard to aviation and automotive transportation were transferred to the newly created Department of Transportation and many of its other functions were consolidated into new divisions each headed by one of the Assistant Secretaries.

The Undersecretary, whose job primarily is to be the Secretary's Deputy, was given a new responsibility in the reorganization, that of heading the newly created United States Travel Service. Around the world today tourism is big business, but it has been essentially the Americans who have been the inveterate travelers, spending millions of American dollars in foreign lands. In the 1960's the United States government became seriously concerned with an adverse balance of payments problem. The United States was spending more money abroad than was being spent by foreigners within her borders. One of the many ways by which the government attempted to solve this financial problem was to establish the United States Travel Service. Its primary task is to entice tourists by publicizing the United States abroad. The Service also encourages American hotel and motel chains, transportation companies, air, rail and bus, and local Chambers of Commerce to offer packaged tours at moderate rates and works to facilitate travel arrangements for foreign visitors. Foreign visitors to the United States not only will contribute to some degree to the solution of the economic problems of the balance of payments, but by coming to the United States will broaden their knowledge of the American people and through understanding them will contribute to international goodwill. The importance attached to this new Travel Service by the government is proved by the fact that the Undersecretary of Commerce supervises the service directly.

The Assistant Secretaries head the four major new divisions of Commerce, each of which contributes to the economic development and the commercial life of the United States. Essentially, the Department of Commerce serves American industry and business by supplying invaluable information on a variety of subjects to enable those concerned to run their affairs more expeditiously. One Assistant Secretary heads the section devoted to Economic Affairs. He works with the Council of Economic Advisers to the President, acting as a liaison between the Department and the White House. He supervises the Office of Business Economics which is mainly a research center to aid American business. Many companies use the statistical reports issued by this office to gauge the business outlook. The monthly magazine, *The Survey of Current Business,* is an invaluable source of business information and helps to take much of the guesswork out of business. This office does a great deal to stabilize American business. This Assistant Secretary also supervises the Bureau of the Census which is one of the most valuable sources of information about every aspect of American life. It is by far the biggest fact-finding agency in the entire government. All the other government offices rely on this bureau to provide them with accurate statistics relating to all aspects of our national life. Originally, census taking was established by the Constitution for the purpose of counting the population for the apportionment of seats in the House of Representatives. The number of Senators is fixed at two, but the number of Representatives is determined according to the population of each State. The Bureau of the Census, therefore, was established to provide, every ten years, an accurate and official count of the people in the United States. From these figures Congress computes the number of representatives to be elected from the States to the Congress of the United States, and the seats are then apportioned among the States according to their respective populations. Since 1790 the Census has been in operation, but over the years its functions have widened to include more than just a population count. Almost every subject is covered by the Census. How many farmers are there? How many businesses? Are certain States losing population? Are others gaining residents? How many babies are born every second? How many people die? How many people immigrate to the United States every year? How many emigrate? How many mothers work? How many children have some sort of employment? There is hardly a statistical question that cannot be accurately answered by the bureau. This service is of great importance not only to the agencies and departments of the federal government, but to the State governments and to citizens everywhere. Though the population count is taken only every ten years, many other surveys are constantly going on, and the bureau is always busy. Much of the information for this service is collected by many employees who walk from door to door asking questions. The material collected is assembled and sent to the central office in Suitland, Maryland, just outside of Washington, D. C., where it is evaluated and made available to any interested person. In recent years the development of the computer has greatly helped the bureau in its work and permits the storage of fantastic amounts of information for future generations of Americans to mull over.

Another Assistant Secretary is responsible for Science and Technology. One of his divisions, the Environmental Science Services Administration, affects the daily lives of every American. This administration, formed in 1965, is made up of five parts, the Environmental Data Service, the Weather Bureau, the Institutes for Environmental Research, the Coast and Geodetic Survey, and the National Environmental Satellite Center. The two best known are the Weather Bureau and the Coast and Geodetic Survey. At first glance it may seem strange to find the Weather Bureau in the Department of Commerce, but, in fact, weather is a determining factor in maritime transportation as well as vital in many other ways to the nation's commercial and agricultural life. Originally, the first weather service was established in 1870 under the Signal Corps of the Army. Later, a weather bureau was set up in the Department of Agriculture, and the service was absorbed by it. In 1940, however, a government reorganization relocated the bureau in the Department of Commerce. The forecasting of the weather is the purpose of the bureau. From its many branch offices all over the United States, Puerto Rico, the Virgin Islands and the far Pacific Islands information is collected. The Air Force also helps the bureau a great deal in this respect. Not only do Air Force planes, equipped with radar and other devices, fly far out over the oceans and detect hurricanes and plot their courses, but Air Force weather satellites far up in outer space also radio back even more detailed information on a global scale. From the reports the weather is then forecast for all parts of the country and the oceans and is then passed on to the public via radio, telephone and television. All storm and flood warnings are issued by the bureau. To air, land and sea travelers these are often lifesaving reports. Weather forecasts are also vital to farmers, and forewarnings of frost, rain or snow can help them save their crops. Practically every citizen has reason to appreciate the Weather Bureau. Motorists are alerted to bad driving conditions; sportsmen are spared the misery of nasty weather; and even picnickers can avoid a wet meal if they heed the weatherman. Aside from the pleasure of the individual, however, weather is one of the most important influences on the commerce of this country, and the Weather Bureau provides one of the most valuable of all government services.

The Coast and Geodetic Survey, now also part of the Environmental Science Services Administration, is one of the oldest offices in the government. As early as 1807 it was established to study the coast of the United States, and in 1878 its work was expanded to include geodetic work. Geodesy is the field of applied mathematics by which exact points in the world and exact sizes and shapes of the earth's surface are determined. No accurate maps can be made without geodetic science. In 1925 the office took over all study on the problems of earthquakes, and with the advent of the airplane, the Survey was given the task of compiling and publishing the aeronautical charts for the civil airways. In 1947 Congress further expanded the Survey by authorizing it to conduct research into all the geophysical sciences. In general, all things of a physical nature affecting the country are the business of the Survey. Maps and charts of local waters, lakes and rivers, earthquake research, studies of geophysical phenomena to aid aerial organization and safety are all the responsibilities of the office.

The Environmental Data Service, the Institutes for Environmental Research and the National Environmental Satellite Center all have to do with the Space Age and the challenges of the unknowns of the universe. Much of the work of these offices is pure research and is directed to helping not only Americans but others around the world plan their daily lives more efficiently by predicting atmospheric conditions so vital to agricultural planning and safety of travel in the air and on the oceans.

Also included among the responsibilities of the Assistant Secretary for Science and Technology are the National Bureau of Standards, the Patent Office and the Office of State Technical Services. The National Bureau of Standards, established in 1901, is primarily responsible for the developing and maintaining of national standards of measurement of physical quantities, such as length, mass, time, temperature, etc. Out of this function has grown another. This essentially scientific Bureau does all the research and development work in the physical sciences for the federal government. In conjunction with this work the bureau is a testing laboratory for all sorts of different materials. It also works with other nations in trying to work out standard systems of measurement for international use. The bureau's services are also available to the States and to private institutions as well as to individuals. If, for instance, a regular bathroom thermometer seems inaccurate, the Bureau of Standards will check it for nothing if the owner sends it to its headquarters just outside of Washington in Maryland. In this way much of its scientific research becomes known and disseminated throughout the country and is of value to each American.

The Patent Office was created in 1790 in order to administer the Patent laws which Congress enacted under Article I of the Constitution. Since then it has been under several departments.

Originally, the Patent Office was located in the Department of State; in 1849 it was transferred to the Department of the Interior; in 1925 it was moved to Commerce by Executive Order of the President, and there it is today. The function of this office is to issue patents for inventions, to administer any federal laws relating to patents and to issue trademarks. It is responsible for determining any questions of priority of invention and the patentability of each invention brought to the office. Until recently the Patent Office was housed in one of the most beautiful buildings in Washington which today houses the National Portrait Gallery and the Museum of Fine Arts, both under the Smithsonian Institution. In a great room under a vaulted ceiling visitors could see every conceivable model of an invention. It was a veritable paradise for those with imagination. Many of the models were successful, therefore patented, and put into production to make life easier, but many were absurd and left to collect dust and to tickle the sense of humor of the curious.

The Office of State Technical Services deals with the fifty States, the District of Columbia, Guam, Puerto Rico and the Virgin Islands, and its job is to encourage economic growth by helping to put scientific knowledge into practical application. It does this by providing funds to local authorized agencies, usually universities, which then work out long-range programs of scientific and technical improvements.

Still another branch of Commerce headed by an Assistant Secretary is specifically devoted to Domestic and International Business. One of the components of this branch is the Business and Defense Services Administration. It serves business by evaluating the effects of modern inventions on business practices and by helping business to take advantage of technological advances. It offers information on international business opportunities to those concerned, on tariff questions, on the impact of imports on the American economy, and handles the obligations of the

United States under the Educational, Scientific and Cultural Materials Importation Act of 1966. The Florence Agreement, as the Act is called, enables specified materials to flow freely between the signatory nations by removing unnecessary trade barriers. In its advisory capacity to the businessmen of the nation, the Administration assists in balancing the distribution of goods and services throughout the land in order to make the most of the productive resources of the country. Small business is one of this office's particular concerns as one of the backbones of the nation's free economy. The Administration also has the important responsibility of carrying out the current programs of the department relating to defense production and plans long-range programs for industrial preparedness in case of war.

On the international side the Assistant Secretary for Domestic and International Business has two major responsibilities. The Office of Foreign Commerical Services works in close partnership with the Department of State in that it is responsible for United States commercial programs abroad. It also advises on the selection of foreign service officers for economic and commercial affairs, evaluates their reports, recommends their assignments, assists in training them for their posts and establishes guidelines governing their responsibilities abroad. The Bureau of International Commerce's task is to promote American business interests abroad and to encourage the export market. This Bureau not only helps American businessmen who trade abroad, but it also promotes American commerce overseas by operating trade centers and by sending American trade expositions to world fairs. A few years ago, for instance, with the help of this office an American supermarket complete to the last detail was transported abroad and was one of the most popular exhibits in an International Fair held in Yugoslavia. Displays of how Americans live go a long way to promote international understanding and goodwill which is as important an aim of this office as the promotion of commerce itself. This Bureau also has the added responsibility of administering the Export Control Act of 1949, which prevents the export of strategic materials and equipment to the Sino-Soviet bloc, and the China Trade Act, which regulates United States exports to Taiwan and Hong Kong.

The fourth Assistant Secretary of Commerce is in charge of the Economic Development Administration which was created in 1965 by Congress through the Public Works and Economic Development Act. This office superseded the earlier office of Appalachian Assistance which had been set up in 1962 in response to the desperate need of the people living in dire poverty in the Appalachian Mountains. The new office has the same mission, to set up long-range programs for the economic development of areas where persistent unemployment exists and the residents live in substandard conditions, but it covers all regions where these conditions are to be found instead of just Appalachia. Federal aid is authorized for areas designated by the Assistant Secretary as qualified, and he works with State authorities in promoting economic development. This office represents still another effort on the part of the federal government to eradicate poverty from the United States and works very closely with the Office of Economic Opportunity and the other allied government agencies concerned with poverty. It is too early to determine whether this office will be entirely successful in eradicating the causes of poverty and in rehabilitating men and women who for too long have lived outside of the American dream, but the fact that the Congress has recognized the problem and has empowered this office within the Department of Commerce to cope with it is at least a step in the right direction.

The many offices which make up the Department of Commerce cannot operate efficiently without management and planning of routine and employees, and the fifth Assistant Secretary for Administration manages the Department for the Secretary. The annual budget for the department's needs is determined by this Assistant Secretary's office. It administers all personnel affairs and supervises all matters necessary to the smooth operation of such a large and diversified department.

Under the Department of Commerce and yet separate from the organization described above is the Maritime Administration headed by an Administrator appointed by the President and confirmed by the Senate. The Maritime Administration is associated with the Department of Commerce because shipping, which has always been important to Americans, means trade and a country's wealth is always greater if it has a large maritime commerce. In wartime also commercial shipping takes on great importance for the transportation of soldiers and supplies to wherever they are needed. Therefore, the government's interest in shipping is great. In the United States merchant shipping is the responsibility of both the Maritime Administration and the Federal Maritime Commission which is an independent agency. The Maritime Administration's main concern is to encourage maritime commerce by investigating and determining ways by which to improve commercial shipping. It also administers all the federal subsidy contracts to private shipbuilding companies and arranges the leasing of United States merchant ships to private concerns. The Administration which is responsible for seeing that the merchant marine is capable of serving as an auxiliary to the Navy in case of war operates the United States Merchant Marine Academy in King's Point, New York. Graduates of the Academy are not only licensed officers in the Merchant Marine, but they are also qualified for commissions as Ensigns in the Naval Reserve. The Federal Maritime Commission does not duplicate the work of the Maritime Administra-

tion. Its principal job is regulatory. The Commission is made up of five members, appointed by the President and confirmed by the Senate who serve for five year terms. Their task is to set rates for water carriers, to set up rules and practices for shippers, to investigate charges of discriminatory rates, and the like. Because the Commission is more of a court and the Maritime Administration is more of a promoter, they do not overlap, but actually complement each other in the task of making the American Merchant Marine first class.

The Department of Commerce, then, has many varied responsibilities. Its overall purpose, however, is to promote a healthy economic life for the nation both at home and abroad by offering diverse services by which American business and commercial life can prosper. In recent years its functions have been expanded to include responsibility for rehabilitating many areas of the country which have suffered privation, and the Department of Commerce now plays its role in the nation's efforts to bring to all citizens the opportunity of sharing in the American dream.

THE DEPARTMENT OF LABOR

Labor is one of the Executive departments whose existence is illustrative of the growth of the nation and of the changing pattern of life in the United States in the last seventy years or so. Until the mid-nineteenth century the United States was a predominantly agricultural land. Though cities, of course, existed, the majority of the population was self-supporting in the rural areas, and most industries were akin to the home type. With the advent of the Industrial Revolution in this country, the way of life for many Americans changed abruptly. With the rise of the factory system a new class of person came into being, the wage earner, the man living in urban communities and totally dependent on his employment in a factory for survival. For many years this working class was ignored by the government. They were not given special consideration by anyone, nor did anyone outside of a handful of humanitarians care about the conditions in which these people worked. In 1884, however, the federal government did become concerned, and in that year official notice was taken of the laboring class by the creation of a Bureau of Labor under the Department of the Interior. As the industry of the United States grew, so did the problems of labor. The

"With the rise of the factory system a

new class of person came into being . . ."

Bureau of Labor was moved out of the Interior Department and became an independent agency without executive rank. In 1903, with the creation of the Department of Commerce and Labor, the Labor Bureau was moved in with Commerce and stayed there until 1913 when a government reorganization recognized the significance of labor and created an independent Department of Labor, the ninth of the Cabinet posts.

The purpose of the Labor Department is to promote the welfare of all the wage earners of the United States. To accomplish this broad assignment, the department is responsible for the administration of federal statutes passed by Congress relating to labor, for the improvement of the working conditions of the laborer and for the advancement of all opportunities for employment. In recent years greater emphasis has been placed on finding ways by which the nation can utilize the abilities of hitherto under-utilized groups, such as women, Negroes, Spanish-Americans and underprivileged youth. Like the other Executive departments, the Labor Department is subdivided into many different offices and bureaus, each with a specific responsibility related to the Department's overall purpose. Heading the organization is the Secretary of Labor, appointed by the President and confirmed by the Senate. Assisting him and responsible for divisions within the Department are an Undersecretary, a Deputy Undersecretary, four Assistant Secretaries, a Commissioner of Labor Statistics, a Solicitor and Directors of offices and bureaus. The Secretary is the President's adviser on labor policy, and his assistants help him in formulating suggested policies and in running and coordinating all the functions under the jurisdiction of the department.

As the problems of unemployment and poverty within the nation have risen to the fore in the last few years, the job of the Assistant Secretary for Manpower has taken on greater importance. In 1953 the Manpower Administration, which is directly under this Assistant Secretary, was created with the primary purpose of mobilizing America's working force in case of national emergency. As much of the nation's security depends on its workers, this office was established in response to the uneasy state of the world in the 1950's. In the 1960's however, the major emphasis of the Manpower Administration is on the development of policies and programs to enable the nation to utilize fully all its manpower resources. The office is charged with formulating programs to erase persistent unemployment and underemployment. It is responsible for developing new educational programs by which to cope with the dislocation of labor due to technological advances such as automation.

To carry out its various responsibilities the Manpower Administration is subdivided into several sections. The Bureau of Apprenticeship and Training has specific responsibilities under the Manpower Development and Training Act of 1965 and works with other government agencies, labor unions, vocational schools and employers to promote apprenticeship and on-the-job training programs to combat unemployment and loss of jobs due to skills becoming obsolete by the technological revolution. The Bureau of Employment Security has many responsibilities. It operates a national system of public employment services and it administers many of the unemployment insurance programs. In carrying out this function the Bureau works closely with the States who may be reimbursed by federal grants for costs incurred in the administering of their unemployment insurance laws. This particular instance is an example of the often close association between the federal government and the States. The Bureau also collects and analyzes data on employment and the national economy and publishes its findings which are available to business, labor unions, educational institutions and, indeed, to any concerned individual. In addition, as another public service it publishes the *Directory of Occupational Titles,* a veritable encyclopedia of jobs available in the nation, and writes job descriptions and occupational tests to help determine the necessary qualifications for different kinds and levels of jobs. This Bureau works in close conjunction with the Office of Economic Opportunity and other government agencies in combatting poverty and works out specific training programs for culturally, educationally and economically deprived youth and runs what amounts to a counseling service for young people in general as well as for veterans seeking to reestablish themselves in civilian life.

Closely associated with this Bureau of Employment Security is the Bureau of Work Programs, also under the Manpower Administration. The principal responsibility of this Bureau is the administration of programs for adults and young people which offer broad ranges of training and career-related services in both rural and urban communities. The Neighborhood Youth Corps, established in 1964, is designed to enable young people of deprived backgrounds to stay in school or return to school by providing them with jobs which give them income and vocational training. Special Impacts, another program under the Bureau, has responsibility for blighted urban areas where poverty with its accompanying tensions is rampant. Practical projects are undertaken to renovate housing, to beautify the neighborhood, to develop recreational facilities, and the like. Both adults and young people who live in the area are hired to carry out the projects, and through employment and cooperation with each other community spirit and pride are instilled in those who otherwise have felt only hopeless discouragement. Operation Mainstream is the third major program in the Bureau of Works Programs, and it, too, is directed at giving the unemployed constructive work particularly in the area of beautification, anti-pollution, and in the improvement and extension of health and social services in urban and rural communities.

New Careers is an innovative, pilot project established in 1966 which seeks to restructure professional jobs in order to better utilize skilled labor. In the area of health services, for instance, New Careers aims at redefining the jobs of nurses and aides. By relieving the Registered Nurse of duties beneath her professional training and assigning them to less skilled aides, two goals are achieved. The nurse is utilized more in keeping with her training and more jobs are made available for the less professionally trained but willing health worker. The same approach is applied to education, and New Careers hopes to open up new jobs for teachers' aides by restructuring the responsibilities and qualifications for teachers. In both cases cited, the beneficiaries are not only those seeking employment, but also the patient in the hospital and the student in the classroom who as a result of the program receive increased personal attention.

The Manpower Administration with all its component parts is one of the most active Offices both in the Labor Department and in the entire federal government in the efforts to extend employment opportunities and give hitherto underprivileged citizens new pride in achievement and new hope for a better life.

Many of the other subdivisions of the Department of Labor are as directly related to the needs of the changing world of the twentieth century as the expanded responsibilities of the Manpower Administration are related to the changing demands and conditions within American society in the 1960's. As the world has grown smaller and international affairs have become vital to national security, the need for an Assistant Secretary for International Affairs was recognized. One of his specific responsibilities is to represent the United States at meetings of the International Labor Organization, and since 1959 when his office was created the Assistant Secretary supervises the work of the Bureau of International Labor Affairs. The responsibilities of this office are broad. The Administrator of the Bureau works directly under the Assistant Secretary for International Affairs and his main job is to follow international labor developments and to analyze their impact on United States foreign and domestic labor policies. The Bureau is divided into geographic areas and the heads of these subdivisions develop action programs for labor interests in foreign countries. They work closely with the State Department to achieve the goals of United States foreign policy abroad through the country programs. As the Department of Commerce works with the State Department on the selection, training and job content of the Foreign Service Officers in the economic and commercial fields, so does this Bureau in the Labor Department work with State in the management of the affairs of the Labor Attachés who serve in the United States embassies abroad. The Bureau is also responsible for United States participation in the United Nations Economic and Social Council and in other international commissions concerned with the problems of labor. The Bureau also develops a reservoir of labor and manpower experts and sets up exchange programs for technical cooperation as well as training programs for foreigners who come to the United States to study the latest developments. The main purpose of this Bureau and the Office of the Assistant Secretary for International Affairs is to advance United States relations with foreign countries by close participation in internationl labor affairs and by the exchange of information with other countries on all issues affecting labor.

In 1963 a reorganization of the Department of Labor consolidated many offices into more efficient units. In that year an Assistant Secretary was put in charge of Labor-Management Relations and under his jurisdiction were placed the Labor-Management Services Administration and the Wage and Hour and Public Contracts Division. The former oversees the operation of welfare and pension plans and the bonding of individuals who handle these plans, investigates complaints registered over these plans, and sees that the laws are complied with. The Labor-Management Services Administration also acts as a watchdog over certain financial and administrative practices of labor unions and sees that elections of union officials comply with the law. Other Offices within this service help industry and labor unions adjust to fundamental changes in the economy and help in arranging for mediators in labor disputes and provide data on labor-management problems to assist mediators in arbitrating specific disputes. Still other sections of this Office do research in labor relations and work with veterans to see that they receive their reemployment rights following periods of active duty.

The Wage and Hour and Public Contracts Division sees that the Fair Labor Standards Act of 1938 and its amendments are carried out. This law sets up the federal minimum wage and hours law for those employed by industries which manufacture goods for interstate commerce and for those engaged directly in interstate commerce. Although the hours and pay rates change periodically, basically the Fair Labor Standards Act states that a worker must work only a limited number of hours for a given amount. Any extra work in overtime is compensated for at a special rate, time and a half, or in other words, half again as much for each overtime hour. This law also places restrictions on child labor. No child under sixteen may be employed in any sort of factory work. No one under eighteen may be employed in any job rated as hazardous by the Bureau, and no child under fourteen may do any sort of work requiring a work permit. This provision means that children under fourteen may work part-time after school babysitting, delivering newspapers, cutting grass or washing cars, but nothing else.

The law also states that any goods manufactured in a place where child labor is used oppressively may not be shipped interstate, and it is the job of this division to see that this statute is rigidly enforced. Restrictions on child labor were a direct outgrowth of the most abusive and offensive types of child employment in the earlier days of the industrial era. These laws regarding the employment of children are among the most beneficial passed by the United States Congress and are strictly enforced by the government. The Wage and Hour and Public Contracts Division has a central office in Washington in the Department of Labor which makes major decisions and interprets various aspects of the law for the entire country. There are also ten regional offices across the United States and overseas which are essentially investigative and report their findings on labor conditions back to Washington where it is assessed and forms the basis for recommendations to the Secretary of Labor for adjustments to the Law. He, in turn, if he agreed that changes were in order, would make his recommendations to the President who then, if he saw fit, would make proposals to Congress.

The fourth Assistant Secretary of Labor is in charge of Labor Standards. His responsibilities cover the Women's Bureau, the Bureau of Labor Standards, the Bureau of Employees Compensation and the Employees Appeals Board.

The Women's Bureau only came into being following the emancipation of women in the twentieth century. Today the role of women in the United States labor force is of great importance. According to the census, approximately one-third of the adult women in the nation hold full-time jobs and another one-third or more work part-time. The Bureau's job is to promote the welfare of all working women and to improve their working conditions. Not only does the Bureau see that women have opportunities for advancement, but it also has the task of seeing that women are not discriminated against in the job market because of sex. Another part of the Bureau's responsibility is to work with international organizations whose aim is to better conditions for women all over the world.

The Bureau of Labor Standards provides many statistical services which are important and helpful to the working people of the country. It compiles and distributes valuable information on the subjects of safety and health regulations in hazardous industries which help to make conditions in those factories better for the employees.

The Bureau of Employees Compensation and the Employees Appeals Board work very closely. The former administers the Workmen's Compensation programs for those employed by the federal government. Loss of a job due to accident or to layoffs is compensated for by the government. The Appeals Board acts as a court in cases of dispute over compensation. It reviews each case presented to it and its judgment is final.

The last three senior officers of the Department of Labor are the Commissioner of Labor Statistics, the Assistant Secretary for Administration, and the Solicitor of the department. The Commissioner of Labor Statistics is the only senior officer of the department who has no enforcement or administrative function. The Office he heads is solely involved in fact-finding and it is the chief source of all information in the field of labor economics. It provides Congress, other Executive departments and agencies as well as the general public with any and all facts that they may require. One of this Office's publications, the *Monthly Labor Review*, is the most authoritative source in the nation on current labor affairs and is widely read by both industry and labor unions.

The Assistant Secretary for Administration has the important and necessary responsibility of running the complicated and vast department. He must see that each of the sections works smoothly, and he, like his counterparts in the other departments, has the task of preparing the budget of the Labor Department for the Secretary. Another of his jobs is to oversee the Library of the Department. This Library contains information on every conceivable subject related to labor and its books and pamphlets are readily available to the general public.

The Solicitor of the department is the chief legal officer and is responsible for all litigation conducted by the department. He is assisted by a large staff of attorneys who are kept extremely busy with the vast amount of legal work that is entailed in carrying out the numerous federal laws related to the American working force.

One thing about the Department of Labor which must be made clear is the fact that it is essentially a labor law enforcement agency as well as a source of information of all aspects of labor in the United States. Although members of the department often work closely with the labor unions of the country, they are in no way connected with them. Labor unions are private organizations made up of wage earners, while the Department of Labor is a government agency set up to serve the wage earners through government policy and planning.

THE DEPARTMENT OF HEALTH, EDUCATION AND WELFARE

The Department of Health, Education and Welfare is one of the more recently established Executive departments. In 1953 a government reorganization agreed to by Congress established the tenth Cabinet post. The purpose behind its creation was to improve the administration of health, education and welfare programs in the United States by centralizing the many offices and agencies in one department. Until 1953 the federal agencies concerned with matters pertaining to these subjects were scattered throughout the government, and, although each was doing a good job, the centralization of policy and direction was deemed necessary. The department is, therefore, an amalgamation of many different agencies and offices under the administration and supervision of the Secretary of Health, Education and Welfare, who is chosen by the President and is confirmed by the Senate. Each office, bureau or agency still has its own head or administrator, and the Office of the Secretary's function is more to supervise and to coordinate overall policies than to run any particular phase of the department. He does have, however, one particular assignment in addition to his overall job, and that is to carry out federal responsibilities toward three federally sponsored corporations, Gallaudet College for the Deaf, Howard University in Washington, D.C., and the American Printing House for the Blind in Louisville, Kentucky. The Secretary is also, naturally, the President's chief adviser on all matters of concern to health, education and welfare.

The Undersecretary and his Deputy assist the Secretary and are largely responsible for the actual running of the organization. Each of the Assistant Secretaries, of whom there are now seven, helps run an aspect of the department.

At the present time under the jurisdiction of the department there are eight separate major offices or agencies, and within their framework there is further subdividing in some cases. The eight are: the Public Health Service (with six subdivisions), St. Elizabeth's Hospital, the Office of Education, the Social Security Administration, the Welfare Administration, the Food and Drug Administration, and the Administration on Aging.

The Public Health Service, which is the oldest of HEW's responsibilities, has had an interesting history. Established originally in 1798, its first and only function was to authorize marine hospitals for American seamen. As medical knowledge has advanced, it has become obvious that good health is as important to a nation as a good economy. Because health is of general concern to everyone, it is natural that the United States government is deeply interested in every field of public health. The overall function of the Public Health Service is to protect and to improve the health of all Americans. To do this, the Service provides opportunities for medical research, for the training of the public in health methods, and also medical and hospital care for those authorized to receive such care out of public funds. The Service also works closely with the States and the governments of other countries in the prevention and control of diseases and in the establishment of community health programs. The Public Health Service is run by the Surgeon General of the United States. His Office supervises all matters concerning general health and correlates the activities in the subdivisions.

In 1966 this Service was reorganized for greater efficiency into the following seven subdivisions: the Bureau of Health Services, the Bureau of Health Manpower, the Bureau of Disease Prevention and Environment Control, the National Institutes of Health, the National Institute of Mental Health, the National Library of Medicine and the National Center for Health Statistics. The last two are actually an integral part of the Surgeon General's office and under his direct supervision. The National Library of Medicine has the greatest collection of medical literature in the world and is constantly used by researchists from the four corners of the earth. It is now housed in a recently constructed building in Bethesda, Maryland, next to the National Institutes of Health, and those who use it are saved hours of laborious pouring through card files compiling bibliographies by MEDLARS, the most up-to-date computerized information storage and retrieval system yet designed. In a matter of minutes all information ever published on arthritis, for instance, can be retrieved by an individual doing research on the disease. The Library also serves as a training center for medical librarians and supports the translation into English of all biomedical literature published abroad. The National Center for

Health Statistics is the most extensive source of information on the actual state of the health of the American people at any given time. From the statistics health forecasts can be made which are useful in that they prepare the medical profession for an outbreak of Asian flu, for instance. The Center also collaborates with the States on the collection of the nation's vital statistics (births, deaths, marriages and divorces) and is the sole source of the tabulation and analysis of the data in the nation.

The other Bureaus in the Public Health Service Administration have divided between them the federal government's responsibilities for the overall health of the nation. The Bureau of Health Services is responsible for improving the quality and availability of health care for all Americans. It provides direct medical and dental care to those eligible to use Public Health facilities (Indians, inmates of federal prisons, the United States Coast Guard, Peace Corps volunteers) and those receiving workmen's compensation under the federal program, in Public Health hospitals and in outpatient clinics. Since the war in Vietnam the Bureau has the additional responsibility for the directing and staffing of the Surgical Team Project under the sponsorship of the Agency for International Development. This Bureau also plans new hospitals and administers the federal grants for their construction and is also charged with the task of developing plans to meet civilian health needs in case of national emergencies. The Bureau of Health Manpower's job is to develop programs for the more effective utilization of health care personnel, to ascertain the nation's need for health workers, and to encourage the nation's young people to seek careers in the health field. The Bureau of Disease Prevention and Environmental Control concerns itself essentially with the prevention and control of communicable diseases, the eradicating of hazards from radiation, air and water pollution, and conducts research into ways of preventing accidental injuries.

Disease can be controlled by quick action, but the prevention of disease in the first place is vital to the improvement of health in the United States. Research, therefore, is one of the most important aspects of medicine. In years past American medicine advanced rapidly due to the foresighted and kind philanthropists like Johns Hopkins who gave their fortunes to further research in medical schools. Today the United States government has taken on as a national responsibility part of the job of providing funds for medical research to benefit all Americans. Some part of the federal funds go to private medical institutions in the country in the form of grants and fellowships to make it possible for them to conduct research. Other funds have created the National Institutes of Health, the government owned research centers operated under the Public Health Service. These institutes, of which there are eight at the moment, deal with the health problems most prevalent in the United States today. They are neurology and blindness, cancer, heart disease, arthritis and metabolic disorders, allergy and infectious diseases, dental research, general medical sciences, and child health and human development. Not only do these institutes have vast laboratories in which experiments and research are carried out, but they also have hospital beds and facilities for patients with unique cases in these fields. Not just anyone may enter the national hospitals. Any doctor who receives an unusual case may get in touch with the institute. If the case is sufficiently special, the hospital may then take the patient. In this way the doctors and scientists of the National Institutes carry on research while curing many ill people.

The National Institute of Mental Health also operates under the Public Health Service, but it is a separate entity from the National Institutes. Its specific mission is to study all forms of mental disorders, to plan constructive programs by which to insure mental health, and to train personnel in the latest techniques to deal with mental illness. It also studies special mental problems such as alcoholism, drug addiction, delinquency and crime, and runs two federal hospitals for drug addicts and alcoholics at Lexington, Kentucky and Fort Worth, Texas.

Although not under the Public Health Service, one of the oldest government owned medical institutions in this country is St. Elizabeth's Hospital for the mentally ill in Washington, D.C. It is administered by the Department of Health, Education and Welfare and is a federally run hospital for the residents of the District, for the beneficiaries of the Public Health Service and for the criminally insane convicted in federal courts.

145

Founded in 1855, this hospital has done research into the causes and possible cures for mental illnesses, and it is an example of the interest in and the responsibility for the welfare of the citizens of this country on the part of the federal government.

Education, since the earliest days of the founding of the Puritan colonies in Massachusetts, has been one of America's principal concerns. No country can be strong, advanced or follow democratic principles without an educated citizenry. That the education offered to Americans be good is of great importance. Public education has traditionally been the privilege and the right of the States and of the local communities within the States. The federal government has never run the public schools of the country, but it has for many years provided much information through research which has been of great use to the States of the Union. The Office of Education, which is now in the Department of Health, Education and Welfare, was first established in 1867. The original purpose of the office was to collect statistics and facts to show the condition and progress of education in the nation. Any information collected was distributed upon request to improve educational systems and to maintain as nearly as possible a standard in the schools throughout the land. Over the years as the country grew, so did the duties of the Education Office. In 1939 the Office was relocated under the Federal Security Agency, but in 1953 with the establishment of the tenth Executive department, it was placed under its jurisdiction.

The Office of Education is the agency of the national government responsible for formulating educational policy and for coordinating educational activities. In recent years its role has been greatly expanded as Congress, urged on by the Chief Executive, has enacted an unprecedented number of laws enlarging the responsibilities of the federal government in the field of education. The staff of the Office works closely with other government agencies, States, professional and citizen groups, as well as with international agencies. The purpose of the office today is to evaluate social and educational trends on a national level, to use these evaluations to improve American educational opportunities and, most importantly, to see that no federal funds, aid or support of any kind go to institutions which discriminate against any American because of race, color, creed or national origin. Educational research and comparative studies of the American educational system with those of foreign countries are also part of the contribution of the Education Office. Although the Office does not administer any of the nation's colleges, it provides research facilities necessary to keep education up-to-date. It is an enormous fact-finding agency, and from its work broad educational policies and programs are devised and implemented.

The third major responsibility of the Department of Health, Education and Welfare is the whole field of social and economic security for many different and disadvantaged segments of American society. The whole concept of social security and welfare is one of the newer responsibilities undertaken by the federal government dating only from 1935. During the days of the great depression in the 1930's many were jobless through no fault of their own. Many older people, who always have more difficulty in finding employment than younger persons, had their savings wiped out and had nowhere to turn for assistance. The idea was then conceived as part of President Roosevelt's New Deal to provide through the federal government a system of social security for Americans to be used for their old age, for times of illness or for periods of unemployment. Security could be made possible by what amounts to government insurance programs. The Act of Congress bringing this idea into reality was the Social Security Act of 1935. By this Act Americans began paying a little each month out of their paychecks to the government, as do their employers. The United States government then matches that sum which, when the employee becomes sixty-five, is given to him in monthly payments, providing his income from all sources is not above a certain figure. Social Security is a retirement sum which gives the worker the promise of security in his older years. Unemployment and disability insurance operates in the same way, only the benefits are received whenever the necessity arises. Through this system, the employer, the employee and the federal government, all three, provide a fund against a time of need, thus making security a reality instead of a dream.

In the 1930's the Office of Social Security was established to administer this program, but very shortly its responsibilities were broadened to include maternal and child welfare. As the population has increased, the problems of modern living have intensified and the role of the federal government over the whole spectrum of social and economic security has had to expand, the administration of Social Security has had to change to keep pace with developments. The first major change occurred in 1946 when the Federal Security Administration was established to oversee Social Security, the Children's Bureau, Old Age and Survivors Insurance, Unemployment Insurance and Public Assistance. This Administration as an independent entity was abolished in 1953 with the creation of the Department of Health, Education and Welfare, which absorbed its work. In 1963 further reorganization within Health, Education and Welfare proved necessary and the Secretary in that year divided the responsibilities for all Social Security between two offices, the Social Security Administration and the Welfare Administration. He gave to the Social Security Administration primary responsibility for retirement programs, Survivors and Disability Insurance and the Federal Credit Unions. The earlier division for Old Age and Survivors Insurance was abolished and the Bureau of Family Services and the Children's Bureau were transferred to the newly created Welfare Administration. In 1965 the Social Security Administration was further reorganized to accommodate "Medicare," a new insurance program enacted by Congress to help the aged with hospital, doctor and other medical bills. In addition to administering the Social Security laws, the Social Security Administration also does research in the areas of poverty and its causes and health care requirements of the aged. From its findings, the Administration is responsible for recommending ways in which these problems resulting from the highly complex society of twentieth century America can best be met by new programs of social insurance. Through the Federal Credit Unions which are cooperative associations the Social Security Administration attempts to encourage the less advantaged in the United States to save money and to practice thrift.

The Welfare Administration now has the responsibility not only for the Bureau of Family Services—which helps the aged, the blind, dependent children, the disabled, and administers "Medicaid," another federal program to help the needy meet medical expenses—and the Children's Bureau—which promotes the welfare of the nation's disadvantaged young—but also for the Office of Juvenile Delinquency and Youth Development and the Cuban Refugee Program. The last two responsibilities reflect new problems which have surfaced to national significance only in the past few years. The Cuban Refugee Program deals specifically, as its title suggests, with the refugees who flee Communist Cuba to Florida. In 1962 Congress, pressed by President Kennedy's personal concern, enacted the Migration and Refugee Assistance Act which finances the basic needs of the Cubans, helps to relocate them, provides funds for medical care and allocates federal funds to the public schools in Dade County, Florida, which have had to expand their facilities not only to take in the Cuban children, but to teach them English so that they can learn. The Juvenile Delinquency and Youth Development Office attempts to prevent delinquency and school dropouts by studying the causes of delinquency and by training people who work in federally supported programs with young people throughout the country.

In the 1963 reorganization of Health, Education and Welfare the old Office of Vocational Rehabilitation was revamped into the Vocational Rehabilitation Administration in order to administer the greatly expanded federal responsibilities in this field. The primary task of this Administration is to improve the methods and opportunities for disabled persons to learn new trades or vocations and by so doing become self-respecting and useful citizens once more. In the past a man or woman who, due to physical disability, lost a job was pretty much finished. Today, through the work of the Vocational Rehabilitation program, many blind, paralyzed or otherwise handicapped persons have received specialized training enabling them to work again. This is one of the most gratifying contributions of the department.

As has been pointed out repeatedly, the federal government keeps restructing itself to be able to meet new problems and to provide solutions for them. In 1965 the President and Congress became aware of a burgeoning problem unique to the latter half of the twentieth century, that of the rapidly increasing number of older citizens within the population of the United States. Advanced medical research, which has conquered many of the age-old killers such as pneumonia, to name one, improved foods, better housing and more recreational facilities have all contributed to enabling people to live longer and well past their working years. As was mentioned above, in 1965 Congress passed the "Medicare" and "Medicaid" laws in recognition of the needs of older Americans for help in meeting hospital bills often for extended stays, in paying for necessary doctors' services and for drugs essential to their health. In the same year Congress passed another law concerning the aged, the Older Americans Act, under which the Administration on Aging was set up within the Department of Health, Education and Welfare. This Administration focuses on all the aspects of the problems besetting the older generation and searches for solutions. It works closely with the States and private institutions in setting up pilot projects and then evaluates their effectiveness. Most of these pilot ventures reflect imaginative thinking and innovative approaches to the problems of the aged. One project, the aim of which is to preclude a feeling of no longer being wanted and intense loneliness, is the Foster Grandparents Program. Older persons without their own relatives are adopted by families and treated literally as honored grandparents. Another project finds employment for the aged poor, not only giving them a little income, but also giving them a sense of purpose. In these ways as well as by the other social and economic measures, the federal government is attempting to insure not only security, but a measure of happiness to those citizens who are past their productive years and who without help might find themselves well outside of the mainstream of American life.

It should be obvious from the above that welfare and health cover many fields. The last major responsibility of the Department of Health, Education and Welfare is that of dealing with the sale of pure foods and drugs. No people can be healthy if bad food or harmful drugs are distributed among them. The Food and Drug Administration in the agency keeps a constant watch over the dinner tables and medicine cabinets of the United States, enforcing federal statutes establishing standards for food and drugs. The federal government first entered into this field in 1906 when widespread appalling conditions in food preparation were disclosed and highly publicized by a group of writers known as the "Muckrakers." In that year Congress passed the Pure Food and Drugs Act which forbade the manufacture and sale of adulterated or unsafe foods or drugs and required the pasting of labels on containers stating the contents. The Food and Drug Administration is the arm of the government responsible for the carrying out of this law and all subsequent related statutes. Today cosmetics, a billion dollar industry, have also been included. Inspectors all over the United States keep a constant surveillance. Much of the work of the Administration is in scientific investigation. Samples of food, drugs, face powders, hair dyes, rinses, and the like are all tested and must be declared safe before they can be sold in the nation. New drugs developed by the chemical and medical supply houses must also pass rigid tests before being adopted. Vaccines for diseases such as polio, which must be made with great care to insure a beneficial reaction, are the special concern of the Administration. Each new batch of vaccine must be tested before it can be distributed to the doctors for use. As many different drug companies are engaged in the manufacture of drugs and vaccines, the job of testing each new batch is a big one, but it must be done for the safety of those who take them.

The Food and Drug Administration is in large part responsible for the high standard of food in the United States and the generally good health of the citizenry. No longer can unsanitary, polluted or spoiled food be sold legally, and the housewife can shop with assurance that what she buys either at the grocery store or at the druggist's is harmless and is what it should be.

The creation of the Cabinet post of Health, Education and Welfare was a valuable addition to the Executive branch. Interest in and responsibility for the welfare of the people of the United States, whether old or young, is as important to the future of this country as a good defense system or a sound foreign policy. Amalgamation of the scattered agencies relating to public welfare into a cohesive whole has resulted in a more efficient and beneficial program for the nation. Its creation also indicates the flexibility of our form of government and is concrete proof of the ability to reorganize for the benefit of the country when the need arises.

THE DEPARTMENT OF HOUSING AND URBAN DEVELOPMENT

Housing and, in fact, all community development in the United States until a few years ago were not concerns of the national government. Quite obviously, with a whole continent before them, generations of Americans simply built homes and cities without government supervision or planning. Interestingly enough, there was only one exception to this rule. Way back in the seventeenth century William Penn, the founder of Philadelphia, was unique in that he was America's first city planner. Before a building was erected in what was to be Philadelphia, Penn had made a master plan in order that the city should be pleasant, safe and uncrowded. The general pattern across the country, however, was that communities just grew helter-skelter, and it was not until very recently that Americans suddenly woke up to the fact that their cities, the heart of the commercial and cultural life of the nation, were absolutely unlivable.

The urban blight which besets the United States today did not begin in earnest until the end of the nineteenth century when the Industrial Revolution swept the country, bringing with it ugly factories and overcrowded slum conditions. Unbeknownst to people of the time, air and water pollution began as sewage, smoke and industrial wastes poured forth into the environment without restraint. As cities grew with the rise of modern America, so did conditions deteriorate commensur-

ately. It was not until the 1930's, however, that national attention was caught by urban problems, and even then it was only
because the depression was so severe that the federal government was forced into recognizing that many Americans lived in
substandard conditions. President Roosevelt's New Deal, therefore, included some legislation for public housing and for financial help for those who needed it to pay for their homes. After
the second World War the federal role was greatly expanded in
the housing field mainly because there simply were not enough
homes for the exploding population of the United States. In the
years since the war because the overall problem of urban and
community development has been aggravated by many other
factors—such as the awareness of air and water pollution, the
civil rights push to eliminate the ghettos, and the gigantic traffic
snarls which tie up every major city in the country during the
rush hours—the federal government has been forced to face up
to its responsibility to the American people to enable them to
live in decent surroundings. Therefore, by request of the President, Congress in 1965 established the eleventh Executive Department of Housing and Urban Development.

This new department, headed by a Secretary, an Undersecretary, a Deputy Undersecretary and five Assistant Secretaries,
was created because, as Congress stated in its Declaration of
Purpose, "the general welfare and security of the Nation and
the health and living standards of our people require, as a matter of national purpose, sound development of the Nation's
communities and metropolitan areas in which the vast majority
of its people live and work." To carry out this responsibility
Congress placed under the jurisdiction of the new department
the previously scattered federal agencies concerned with various aspects of housing and urban affairs, the Housing and
Home Finance Agency, the Federal Housing Administration,
the Public Housing Administration and the Federal National

Mortgage Association. The Secretary with his assistants now coordinates the work of these offices and, in addition, encourages the finding of solutions for housing and urban problems through research. He works with the States and local communities for interstate and regional cooperative plans and with private construction interests to promote programs for urban renewal and for low and moderate cost housing.

The department really has two functions, to devise new ways by which old communities can be improved and rehabilitated and by which new communities can be built to enhance the lives of their inhabitants, and to provide financial help to States and to cities to enable them to launch their immensely costly renewal projects. The latter responsibility is largely that of the Assistant Secretary for Mortgage Credit and Federal Housing Commissioner. The Federal Housing Administration, which is under this Assistant Secretary, carries out loan and mortgage insurance programs for specified projects, for home improvement, for urban renewal, for areas struck by disaster such as hurricane or flood, for rental units such as motels, for nursing homes, for housing for members of the armed services, for group medical facilities and for experimental housing. The other Assistant Secretaries each help to carry out the other function, that of devising new cures for the already existing urban blight. The Assistant Secretary for Renewal and Housing Assistance oversees slum clearance and certain kinds of urban renewal projects. He is charged with providing what is called open space land in urban areas, for beautification projects, and with planning for orderly community redevelopment by relocating industries, for instance, away from residential areas. The Assistant Secretary for Metropolitan Development has among his concerns the acquisition, restoration and preservation of historic sites, and the Assistant Secretary for Demonstration and Intergovernmental Relations directs among other things the Model Cities Program under which cities can receive federal funds if they present imaginative and innovative plans for renewal projects.

One point must be emphasized about the role of the new Department for Housing and Urban Development. It is not designed to dictate to the cities or to take over authority from the city governments, but it is rather a center for the coordination of programs for urban renewal and planning and exists primarily to help communities as well as individuals help themselves to live better lives in more attractive and healthier surroundings. The department only began operations in 1966, and it is too soon to judge whether it will be successful in revolutionizing the nation's cities and bringing an end to urban blight. The approach, however, that the department is taking, to examine and consider all aspects of city life, water, air, sewage, industry, business, residence, transportation and recreation, is positive, and the probability is that federal participation in what amounts to a national housecleaning will result in constructive change. William Penn would probably be vastly amused as well as a little saddened to know that it has taken the United States almost three hundred years to realize that city planning has its value and that "an ounce of prevention is indeed worth a pound of cure."

THE DEPARTMENT OF TRANSPORTATION

Nothing is more vital to the well-being and prosperity of the United States today than rapid, efficient and safe transportation. In 1966 the Congress of the United States, in recognition of this fact, established the twelfth department in the Executive branch, the Department of Transportation, ordering it to begin serving the American people in April, 1967. Very much like the Department of Health, Education and Welfare, the Department of Transportation was not created entirely out of whole cloth nor was it given many new duties, but it was set up to place under one roof all the already existing agencies and commissions scattered throughout the government concerned with all the various forms of transportation in existence today. The establishment of this new department, therefore, caused major reorganizations among the older departments as they lost responsibilities to Transportation. The purpose of the new department is to provide fast, safe, efficient and convenient transportation at the lowest possible cost for the American people. By having control over all modes of transportation centered in one place and under the jurisdiction of the Secretary of Transportation, the people of the United States stand to benefit by the coordination of policies and by the concentrated emphasis on technical advances that result from centralization.

The new department, like all the others, is administered by the Secretary, the Undersecretary, the Deputy Undersecretary, five Assistant Secretaries and the General Counsel. These top officials differ from their counterparts in the other departments in that they do not administer the components of the department. They are responsible instead for coordinating all policies, for public relations, for international affairs and for research and technology. Each agency which was transferred to the Department of Transportation retained its own structure and is still headed by its officials.

There are six components of Transportation, five transferred intact from other parts of the government and one newly established, the National Transportation Safety Board. This Board is made up of five members appointed by the President and confirmed by the Senate for five year terms. These men are responsible for both aviation and surface (rail, highway, marine and pipeline) safety. Their job is to investigate all accidents, to determine the probable cause and to make recommendations on the basis of their findings to prevent further mishaps. They also handle the appeals in cases in which licenses or certificates to operate airplanes or other kinds of transportation have been suspended or revoked. The other five agencies within the Department of Transportation are the United States Coast Guard, the Federal Aviation Administration, the Federal Highway Administration, the Federal Railroad Administration and the St. Lawrence Seaway Development Corporation.

The United States Coast Guard was transferred from the Department of the Treasury where it had been since 1915. It may seem odd that a maritime unit was in the Treasury, but the nature of many of its duties made it logical for the service to be in the Treasury in peacetime alongside of the Bureau of Customs until the Department of Transportation was created. The Coast Guard is one of the largest of the law enforcement agencies in the country. It is responsible for the enforcement of all federal laws on the waters under the jurisdiction of the United States government. The Coast Guard sees that all laws regarding ship inspection and navigation are carried out. The Coast Guard is responsible for enforcing the revenue, customs and immigration laws. Though wildlife is protected by a division of the Department of the Interior, it is the Coast Guard that protects sea wildlife and carries out the conservation measures deemed necessary by other sections of the government. In Alaska it used to be the members of the Coast Guard who were appointed as United States Marshals to carry out the law. Also, the security of ports and the safety of ships at sea are part of the Coast Guard's responsibilities. To accomplish the latter, the Service maintains lighthouses and lifesaving stations along the coasts of the nation; it clears waters of derelicts and other objects dangerous to shipping; it efficiently patrols the northern sea routes, smashing up ice blocks and keeping an eye out for icebergs. The Coast Guard is also one of the chief sources of information on the broad subject of oceanography and its vessels conduct research as they patrol the waters bordering the United States. The Service also since 1960 has regulated the pilotage on the Great Lakes, maintaining a pool of pilots and setting rates and charges for their services.

Should war break out, the Coast Guard automatically becomes part of the Navy, whose primary task is to defend the United States militarily on the oceans against the enemy. The members of the Coast Guard are well equipped to become part of the Navy. The Coast Guard Academy in New London, Connecticut, is much like the Naval Academy in Annapolis, Maryland, and its graduates are expert sailors. In peacetime, however, the law-enforcing role of the Coast Guard and its services to those who sail the nation's waters explain its position in the Department of Transportation.

The Federal Aviation Administration, formerly an independent agency, has the responsibility to regulating all air commerce in the United States to keep it safe, efficient and prepared, if necessary, for a role in national defense. The Administration also encourages the development of civil aeronautics, controls all the air lanes, assigning different ones to airlines, and develops and operates the systems of air traffic control within the United States. In conjunction with its responsibilities for the safety of air traffic, the FAA conducts all examinations and certification of pilots and inspections of aircraft to make sure that they comply with the latest United States safety standards. It is also charged with research on supersonic transport aircraft and works closely with the aviation industry to produce a safe and economically feasible plane. As air travel becomes more and more popular, the FAA has an increasingly difficult job to perform. Everyone wants to fly, and to meet the demand the commercial airlines keep putting more and more planes in the air. Airports, particularly in the eastern United States, are becoming terribly overcrowded and the danger of accidents keeps mounting. It is the Federal Aviation Administration which must try to satisfy the ever growing demand for speedy air service and at the same time insist that at all times the safety of the air passengers is the first consideration.

The Federal Highway Administration took over the jobs formerly performed by the Bureau of Public Roads in the Department of Commerce and the Corps of Engineers of the United States Army. This Administration is now responsible for all the existing interstate, federally funded highways across the United States and for planning the construction of new ones deemed necessary. Another primary responsibility of this Office is to coordinate highways with the other modes of transportation to achieve the best balance of systems for the United States for peacetime and, most importantly, for defense purposes in case of war. In today's world in which the quality of life has become a national concern beautification of the highways is another important consideration of the Highway Administration. Not only are billboards excluded from new federal highways, but the engineers who design them now make every effort not to mar the beauty of the landscape through which the roads must pass. This Administration is also extremely concerned with automotive safety, and it establishes and enforces national standards for the operation and performance of motor vehicles. Tire manufacturers come under their jurisdiction also, and they must label pneumatic tires, for instance, so that purchasers know that they conform to federal standards. The Highway Administration also operates a central national register for auto licenses that have been revoked or suspended for violations of highway safety codes. No longer can an offender leave a State and operate a motor vehicle with impunity elsewhere. The Administration maintains a strict surveillance on all interstate trucking and inspects the machines, removing those that are in hazardous condition from service.

Lastly, the Administration is constantly working to improve driver education programs and, like the Federal Aviation Administration, investigates accidents on the highways and attempts to eradicate the causes to prevent further tragedies. This Administration ought to be better known than it is because its work is solely in the interest of the millions and millions of car and truck owners who too often use the nation's highways recklessly. The Highway Administration can only make the nation's roads as safe as modern engineering allows. The rest is up to the American behind the wheel.

The fourth component of the Transportation Department is the Federal Railroad Administration which in 1967 took over the activities of the old Bureau of Railroad Safety and Service from the Interstate Commerce Commission, the Office of High Speed Ground Transportation from Commerce, and the operation of the Alaska Railroad from Interior. The overall purpose of this Administration is to establish uniform safety standards, to encourage railroad development and to ascertain the nation's railroad requirements for the future. The last two tasks are rather difficult today because automotive and air transportation have almost succeeded in supplanting the railroads as a mode of travel and as a way of shipping freight. In the past few years one railroad after another has gone out of existence, and the few remaining once great lines such as the Pennsylvania and the New York Central have had to merge in order to survive. The great hope for railroads now lies in the high speed trains which are still in the experimental stage. If they can be perfected, they will be of inestimable value to the crowded sections of the United States. Today on the eastern seaboard, for instance, almost everyone wishing to go to Washington from Boston or New York will choose to fly rather than to go by train. The train takes hours and the plane, minutes. The air lanes, however, have become so jammed that all too often planes are forced to circle for long periods before they can receive permission to land from the control tower at the airport. When the new trains are in service, many will prefer to take them instead of flying not only because of their high speed but also because of the convenient access to them. Train terminals are without exception in the heart of metropolitan areas whereas airports are generally far out in the country, and the busy businessman will find that he is actually saving time by traveling on the high speed lines. The Federal Railroad Administration has assigned a high priority to the High Speed Ground Transportation program and as soon as it is technically feasible these new trains will be in service. Another duty of this Administration, that of operating the Alaska Railroad, is unique as it is the only instance in the entire government, apart from the Armed Forces, in which a government office actually runs a service. The Alaska Railroad differs from the other lines in the United States because it is a government built and operated line. Its primary function is to encourage the settlement and economic development of the State and for that purpose it maintains 482.7 miles of main track from Seward to Portage Junction with spur lines along the way. This line, though operated by the Federal Railroad Administration, has its tariffs set by the Interstate Commerce Commission which also sets the rates for all the privately owned lines in the country. One other responsibility of the Railroad Administration is interesting in that it reflects the days when railroading was in its infancy and was extremely hazardous. The Administration still has the duty of selecting candidates for the Medals of Honor which are awarded by the department to those who risk their lives while saving others from wrecks or other major disasters.

The last unit under the Department of Transportation is the St. Lawrence Seaway Development Corporation. This corporation was established by act of Congress in 1954 and its purpose is to construct the part of the St. Lawrence Seaway between Lake Ontario and St. Regis, New York, which is in United

States territory. The corporation also works closely in this enterprise with the Canadian government with whom the St. Lawrence Seaway project was conceived. The seaway is one of the most constructive of all government projects going today in that when it is completed, deep water navigation will be possible all the way up to the Great Lakes, bringing much more shipping into the heart of the continent, and there will also be a great deal more hydroelectric power available to both Canadians and Americans which will improve their standard of living. The tolls paid to the corporation by the shippers using the seaway will pay for the tremendous cost of building it and will eventually make the corporation profit-making.

The Department of Transportation, the latest to join the Executive branch, will undoubtedly grow immeasurably in the future as advances are made in the modes by which men travel. Helicopters, for instance, may become as common as the automobile, and if they do, the regulation of their traffic and the safety standards for their operation will become the responsibility of this department. It is also not inconceivable that the Secretary will find himself one day regulating interplanetary travel. In the meantime, Americans who are the most mobile people on earth are protected to the best of the government's ability by the Department of Transportation's careful monitoring of the present-day means of getting from one place to another.

The Development of the Legislative Branch

In 1787 when the Constitution was written, the framers of the document created a plan for the United States Congress or the Legislative branch. Each of its two houses was given responsibilities, officers and an organizational plan. As the years have passed, the Legislative branch has changed and expanded in much the same manner as has the Executive branch. Some of the changes are organizational due to enlarged membership, others have to do with the addition of responsibilities. The size of Congress has expanded since 1789. The first Congress was made up of Senators and Congressmen from only thirteen States. Today there are fifty States in the Union, sending one hundred Senators and four hundred and thirty-five Representatives to Washington for each session of Congress. Another change which has taken place since 1789 is the manner in which Senators are elected. Originally, the Constitution provided for the election of Senators by the State Legislatures. In 1913 a constitutional amendment changed this system, replacing it with the direct election of Senators by the citizens of each of the States in the Union.

As the numbers in Congress have grown, the organization of the Legislature has been adapted to handle the greater membership. Both the Senate and the House have added officers to those mentioned in the Constitution to perform duties pertinent to the efficient running of Congress. Although the Vice-President is still the President of the Senate as prescribed by the Constitution, and the Senate still elects a President Pro Tempore from its membership in case of the absence of the Vice-President or his elevation to the Presidency, two other Senate positions have been created. The Secretary of the Senate is elected by the Senate, and his task is varied. Should the Vice-President be absent and a President Pro Tempore of the Senate conceivably have not yet been elected, the Secretary of the Senate would perform the duties of the head of the Senate. To date, this situation has never arisen. The Secretary is the Custodian of the Seal of the United States Senate. He draws money from the United States Treasury to pay the Senators. He is responsible for administering all oaths to officers of the Senate or to witnesses who appear before that body. He also certifies the ratification of peace treaties and the confirmation of nominees by the Senate to the President of the United States.

To keep order in the Senate and in the Capitol building, the position of Sergeant at Arms was established. Elected by the Senate, the Sergeant at Arms manages the Capitol police and the doorkeepers. It is he who collects a quorum of Senators (the minimum number required by law to do business), when directed to, and his presence is required at all sessions of the Senate.

In the House of Representatives the position of Clerk of the House has been created to perform certain duties important to the efficiency of that body. The Clerk has a continuing job from Congress to Congress. He presides over each new session of Congress until the Speaker of the House is elected. He is the Keeper of the House Seal, and he prepares the roster of all Representatives duly elected to the House. He also witnesess all bills, resolutions and subpoenas for the House.

These officers of Congress, in addition to those mentioned in the Constitution, perform the practical tasks necessary to the smooth functioning of the Legislative branch of the government. Without them the important legislative responsibilities of Congress would be difficult to carry out.

Another system which has no constitutional foundation, but has developed over the years in Congress to help carry out its functions with greater dispatch, is that of the committees. The Constitution lists carefully the responsibilities of lawmaking for both the House and the Senate, but nowhere does it state how these responsibilities should be carried out. With the increased number of members in both houses, it would be almost impossible for each law necessary to the country to be proposed, discussed and formulated by all members at one time. Were that

A Congressional committee in session

the system, each law would take an unconscionable length of time to be enacted. To avoid such delays, the committee system was devised. In both the House and the Senate there are standing committees on various subjects whose job it is to prepare legislation for consideration by the full membership. In this manner all legislation pertaining to foreign affairs, for instance, is originated, debated and prepared in the proper legislative form by members of the Foreign Affairs committee. Time is saved, and when the bill is in its final form it is then presented to the House or the Senate and is either passed or tabled. In the Senate there are sixteen regular committees and in the House, twenty. At any time, however, either house may appoint special committees if necessary to investigate any situation pertaining to the legislative function of Congress. At each new session of the Congress the two houses set up their standing committees. The leaders of the two largest political parties, the Republican and the Democratic, hold meetings of their party members and apportion the chairmanships of the committees. The politics of the chairmen of the committees always indicate which political party is in the majority in each session of Congress. The seniority rule prevails in the allotment of the chairmanships. The men who have served the most consecutive terms in Congress are those who get the chairmanships of the most important committees. Membership on the committee is awarded also by the seniority system. A man elected for the first time to either the Senate or the House would, therefore, be on a committee of less importance than one who returned after many terms. When the political parties have chosen their chairmen and members of the committees, the appropriate house of Congress then must approve the choices. The special committees are organized in the same way as the standing committees, but operate only for a limited period of time. Should there be a need for their continuing, whichever

house has set them up must vote the continuance.

Congress has responsibilities apart from its legislative function and it must supervise several organizations which have been placed by law under its jurisdiction. The Architect of the Capitol, the United States Botanic Garden, the General Accounting Office, the Government Printing Office and the Library of Congress have all been created by Act of Congress since 1789 and are still supervised by Congress today.

In 1793 the Architect of the Capitol was appointed in order to build the Capitol building. Now the Architect maintains and supervises not only the Capitol, but adjacent buildings also. It is his job to care for the Supreme Court, the Congressional Office buildings, the Library of Congress and the United States Court of Claims building. Any maintenance problems or new buildings required for Congress come under his jurisdiction. He also supervises the Capitol grounds.

In 1820 the Columbia Institute for the Promotion of Arts and Sciences constituted the first botanic garden. In 1837, however, this institute was abandoned, and botanical interest flagged. In 1842 a United States Exploring Expedition to the South Seas caused a reopening of the botanic garden because it sent many botanical specimens to Washington. Hastily a greenhouse was built to take care of the plants and was placed under the Joint Congressional Committee on the Library for want of a better place. From that humble beginning the present Botanic Garden grew. Originally its purpose was to collect and to grow plants of domestic and foreign sorts for medical and horticultural interest. Today the Botanic Garden is mainly a place for the exhibition of all kinds of plants. The garden provides material for garden clubs and groups and for students of botany. The staff will also identify any plant from any place in the world for an interested person. The Garden no longer performs any real scientific purpose, but is an interesting place for all who enjoy plants and unusual garden effects.

The Library of Congress performs to this day an important task in education for the whole country. In 1800 five thousand dollars were appropriated by Congress to establish a library purely for the use of the members of Congress. It was thought important to have material at hand for lawmakers to help them in their task. From that limited beginning the Library of Congress has grown into what is really a library for the nation. It is one of the greatest libraries in the world. Not only does it have literary material on every conceivable subject, but it is the largest repository of American first editions as it is the official register of all copyrights in the United States. The Library also houses a national collection of music and photographs of interest to the country. Recently, the Library has provided the "talking books," recordings of literary works for the blind. Any adult can avail himself of the Library, and for those who cannot come to Washington, material can be loaned through public and private libraries throughout the land. Although the Library has come to include many services never thought of in 1800, it still performs the specific function of helping members of Congress through the Legislative Reference Service. This Service makes available to Congressmen all material pertinent to any legislation under consideration and provides one of the most valuable services in Washington. The Library is headed by a Librarian appointed by the President and confirmed by the Senate. Generally this position is filled by an outstanding poet, writer or educator of the nation. It is a position of honor. The Library represents one of the outstanding educational functions of the federal government and is of value today to all Americans instead of just to the members of Congress whom it nevertheless continues to serve.

The General Accounting Office and the Government Printing Office are the other two organizations run by Congress. The Accounting Office performs an independent audit of all government finances in order to facilitate the payment of government bills and to be sure that the enormous government expenditures are kept in order. This Office is a method of controlling the exercise of the exclusive power of Congress to appropriate funds for government projects. The Government Printing Office prints all government records and documents as well as distributing and selling them to interested persons. Also, this Office supplies every government office with paper, ink, pens and other materials upon request.

The creation of these Offices reflects the changes in American life since 1789 and necessities arising from these changes. Congress still performs the lawmaking tasks assigned to it by the Constitution, but the manner in which the legislative responsibility is carried out has evolved over the years.

The Independent Agencies

The Executive, the Legislative and the Judicial branches of the federal government were designed to provide for an effective government for the United States. Since 1787, however, as the size and the responsibilities of the federal government have increased, there have been established other government commissions, agencies and boards in Washington which are not subordinate to any of the three major constitutional branches. Each originated due to a specific need, and each was created by an Act of Congress and granted specific powers. Congress set up these extra-constitutional agencies as the most efficient way to provide management and regulation for problems pertaining to all Americans which no existing part of the government was equipped to handle. There are, in general, two kinds of these organizations, the independent agencies and the quasi-official agencies.

The independent agencies are many and cover a wide variety of subjects, each important to some aspect of American life. They are called independent because, although their heads must be appointed by the President and confirmed by the Senate, the agencies are not under the immediate jurisdiction of either the White House or the Congress in the execution of their jobs. In general, these agencies make independent regulations and decisions pertaining to their responsibilities, some to a greater extent than others. Some of the main independent agencies are as follows: the Atomic Energy Commission, the National Aeronautics and Space Administration, the Federal Communications Commission, the Federal Trade Commission, the Federal Reserve Board, the Federal Power Commission, the Interstate Commerce Commission, the National Labor Relations Board, the Securities and Exchange Commission, the General Services Administration, the Veterans' Administration and the Smithsonian Institution. As their names suggest, each is created to deal with a definite and specified task. Each represents on the part of Congress a decision to allot to a group the functions of a part of the task of regulating our national life. Were Congress to attempt to manage every aspect of American life, its job would be hoplessly bogged in detail. This partial list of the independent agencies of the federal government illustrates an historical method of solving problems arising with new developments in America. A description of the Atomic Energy Commission, the Federal Trade Commission, the General Services Administration and the Smithsonian Institution, each an agency with differing degrees of independence and authority and each with a different purpose, will serve to explain the manner in which these agencies work and the reason for their being.

During World War II atomic scientific research and development for war purposes were conducted by the United States Army under the direction of the Corps of Engineers. In cooperation with our allies during the war, atomic energy was harnessed, and atomic bombs were developed and manufactured. With the famous explosions in 1945 at Hiroshima and Nagasaki in Japan, the news of atomic energy was released for the world. After the war the question of how to control and develop atomic energy for peacetime as well as for defense purposes was raised. At the time all atomic resources were government controlled. Americans, however, have always believed in free enterprise in business. Should the United States government or the private businessmen of the nation develop this new form of power? Many factors made a solution to this problem difficult. The compelling necessity of controlling the production and use of fissionable material for weapons required the government to retain close regulation over this industry. The fact that atomic research had been conducted in cooperation with foreign allied countries during the war further complicated the problem. Whereas the United States government through the Department of State is in a position to deal officially with foreign nations, private companies would not be. The question after much debate was finally answered by the United States Congress, and the decision of what to do about atomic energy was taken in the Atomic Energy Act of 1946. This Act stated that in the future all matters pertaining to atomic energy should be controlled by a United States Atomic Energy Commission whose purpose it would be to make United States policy relating to atomic energy for the maximum contribution to American defense and general peacetime welfare. A Commission of five men was set up to make policy and programs and to administer the development of atomic research. Thus, with the establishment of this Commission, every matter relating to atomic energy was brought under one jurisdiction. Private citizens, scientists, the State Department, the Defense Department . . . all deal with this one Commission. It is the responsibility of the five commissioners to see that atomic programs are efficiently carried out. But, as atomic weapons are of such significance and importance to national defense and to foreign affairs, the Secretaries of Defense and State, as well as the President of course, have much to do with decisions regarding atomic policy. In this respect the Atomic Energy Commission, though called an independent agency, is, in fact, controlled by the Executive branch. Policies for the peacetime development of atomic energy, however, are the sole responsibility of the commissioners, and in that field they operate independently.

The Federal Trade Commission is an example of the truly independent agency. The Commission regulates trade practices of private business and acts in a quasi-judicial way. Quasi means to a certain degree. The agency, therefore, acts as a court and makes decisions on its own concerning matters before it. Because of the nature of its work, the Commission is set up in a way somewhat similar to that of an Executive department. There are various bureaus which function under the five commissioners who head the Commission.

The Federal Trade Commission was founded in 1915. Its authority was derived originally from two Acts of Congress, the Federal Trade Commission Act and the Clayton Act, both passed in 1914. The purpose of both acts was to maintain the American system of free enterprise in business and to prevent unfair competition or deceptive trade practices. Since 1915 many other Acts of Congress have enlarged its jurisdiction. The Export Act, the Wool Products Labeling Act, the Fur Products Labeling Act, the Flammable Fabrics Act and the Lanham Trademark Act have each added a new function to the Trade Commission's job. The Commission carries out these laws in specific ways. The Commission sees that free and fair competition in interstate commerce is maintained by preventing price fixing arrangements, agreements or boycotts, by preventing combinations whose purpose it is to restrain free trade, and by stopping all unfair or deceptive practices of any sort. The Commission safeguards the public by checking for misrepresentations all advertisements of foods, drugs, cosmetics or therapeutic gadgets. Although all advertisements exaggerate to some extent, they may not mislead the purchaser either in a manner dangerous to him or in a manner calculated to cheat him. Any form of price discrimination, exclusive dealings or tie-in sales are strictly forbidden in the interest of free enterprise. The Commission also forbids the mergers of corporations should such combinations be of monopolistic purpose or effect. All fur and wool garments must be properly and honestly labeled to guard the public from fraud. A mink must be a mink and not a dyed muskrat. With the introduction of synthetic fabrics, the Commission has taken on the job of protecting the public against flammable materials. Some of the synthetic yarns, at first, turned out to be highly dangerous in that they would unexpectedly burst into fire, burning the unsuspecting user badly. The Commission prevents the sale of any such dangerous fabrics. The Commission also receives and deals with petitions for the cancellation of false trademarks, thereby protecting the consumers from fraudulent products.

The Commission carries out its functions by issuing "cease and desist" orders to companies or individuals who break any of the trade laws. Although the Commission has legislative and judicial functions, it cannot punish offenders. If any infractor refuses to comply with the "cease and desist" order, the offender is then brought to justice in either a United States district court or an appellate court. Not in every case is an order necessary. The Commission carries out much of its work by voluntary compliance. The Commission discovers an infringement and points it out to the culprit who in many instances willingly stops the offending practice. The "cease and desist" orders are for those who refuse to obey voluntarily.

The volume of work of the Commission necessitates a large and well-organized staff. The Commission is headed by five members who are appointed by the President and confirmed by the Senate, each for seven years. No more than three members can be of the same political affiliation at one time. From the five the President appoints a chairman. Serving under the Commissioners are several bureaus, each responsible for a specific aspect of the Commission's work. The Investigation Bureau is charged with the responsibility of discovering violations of any federal trade statute. The Bureau of Litigation carries out any trial work. The Bureau of Consultation works to get voluntary compliance with the laws. When a "cease and desist" order is issued, trial examiners hear the cases. Their decisions become the decisions of the Commission unless the case is appealed for review before the five commissioners or if the commissioners decide that they want to look into the case themselves. The Bureau of Economics provides all the research necessary for the work of the whole Commission. Under the five commissioners and supervisor of all the Bureaus is an Executive Director. He is responsible for the general administration of the Commission. The General Counsel of the Commission is its legal adviser on questions of law, policy and procedure. The Secretary of the Commission is the Custodian of the Seal and handles all papers and records as well as the mail. He signs all orders issued by the Commission, keeps the calendar and writes the minutes of each session.

Cases come to the Federal Trade Commission through its own investigation department or on appeal by either individuals or companies. Anyone who detects an infringement of a trade law and reports it to the Commission is guaranteed secrecy. The name of a person who complains is never disclosed. He may produce his evidence or he may ask the Commission to investigate a situation without concrete proof of an infringement. If the violation is real, and there is no voluntary compliance, and a "cease and desist" order is ignored, the United States Justice Department takes over the case and the offenders are punished by fines, jail terms or both. Free enterprise is guaranteed for all Americans by this Commission and rarely does a scheme to defraud the public go undetected.

The General Services Administration operates in a different way from either the Federal Trade Commission or the Atomic Energy Commission because the nature of its responsibilities are different. In 1949 a government reorganization created the General Services Administration. Its title suggests its purpose. The Administration performs many services all necessary for the federal government. All procurement of real estate needed by the government and all disposal of property no longer needed are part of the functions of this agency. All maintenance, improvements and designs for federal office buildings, with the exception of those specifically assigned to the Architect of the Capitol, are the responsibility of General Services. The National Archives of the government are also under its supervision. All the records, papers, documents, etc., of the many offices of the federal government are gathered, filed and made available to the public through this department. Another of the functions of the Administration is to regulate and to arrange for all government transportation and utilities in Washington and in all other federally controlled areas. The Administration's tasks are varied. It acts as a general coordinator of all the government's housekeeping chores, and it is headed by an Administrator with many assistants. The General Services Administration works closely with the White House and the Executive departments in its job of taking care of the details of housekeeping so necessary to the smooth running of the government.

The Smithsonian Institution is an independent agency of an entirely different nature from the three just described. The Smithsonian Institution is really a national museum and zoological park. It was set up in 1846 by Congress under the terms of a will of one James Smithson of London, England, who left a sizeable amount of money to the United States government for "an establishment for the increase and diffusion of knowledge among men." To this gentleman Americans of all ages owe a tremendous debt. The Smithsonian in Washington contains thousands of exhibitions all fascinating to students of Americana. Every facet of our national life is represented in one of the museums under the Institution's direction. The history of the development of the navy, the air age, the American Indians, the clothes of every era, the growth of the Industrial Revolution, the animal and bird life of the western continents . . . all these subjects and many more can be found at the Smithsonian. For the lover of fine arts, the Freer Gallery of Oriental Art, the National Gallery of Art, the National Collection of Fine Arts, and the National Portrait Gallery offer unique and valuable exhibitions. These museums were not, however, part of the original bequest. The National Gallery of Art was the gift to the American people of Andrew Mellon, and the Freer Gallery, the gift of the Freer family of Detroit. In recent years Congress authorized the new Collection of Fine Arts and the National Portrait Gallery.

The National Zoological Park is another branch of the Institution and a favorite among children. In Rock Creek Park in Washington the Smithsonian maintains a zoo filled with interesting specimens of live animals and birds from all parts of the world.

The Smithsonian is not only a museum, but it also is a source of information for anyone interested in identifying objects of animals or for students of any of the many subjects under its jurisdiction. Today the Smithsonian is supported by funds supplied by the government, the original bequest having long since been exhausted. Each of the many bureaus under the Institution has its own head, but the Smithsonian is directed by a board of regents made up of the Chief Justice of the United States, the Vice-President, two Senators, three members of the House of Representatives and five outstanding citizens of the United States. The Smithsonian Institution is an example of government in the educational and pleasurable side of national life and is one of the most fascinating of all federal projects.

These four independent agencies have been singled out for discussion only because they represent widely differing functions. Each of the many other independent agencies operates more or less in the same general pattern, but each naturally has a specific function. The Federal Communications Commission is organized, for instance, to deal with radio and television development in the United States. Its purpose is to regulate the air waves so that the maximum benefit possible from radio and television is brought to the American people. The Interstate Commerce Commission regulates all trade between the fifty States. The Federal Power Commission is responsible for the regulation of forms of power in the country with the exception of atomic power. Gas and hydroelectric power come under its supervision. The Civil Service Commission regulates and makes decisions, subsequent to the President's direction, concerning the thousands of United States government employees. The Veterans' Administration supervises all matters relating to the Veterans' Acts passed by Congress.

Some of these independent groups appear to have overlapping responsibilities with bureaus in the Executive departments. But although the offices in the Executive branch work closely with the agencies, their jobs are not similar. The Offices in the Executive departments work mainly in an advisory and research capacity. The distinction is that the independent agencies make regulations and decisions pertaining to their field and enforce them on their own authority. The use of the word independent, of course, does not mean that these agencies are entirely separated from the rest of the government. The Senate confirms the members of the commisssions and each agency is required to file a report either once or twice a year with Congress. Also the power of Congress to institute special investigations means that the commissions' work can be closely followed by the interested committee in Congress. Congress has the sole power to appropriate money for the operation of the agencies, and that power over the purse strings is a strong rein on the work of the commissions. In general, though, the agencies operate in regulatory and independent capacities. All problems concerning their particular subject come under their jurisdiction, and they manage their affairs pretty much as they see fit.

The quasi-official agencies are of an entirely different nature from the independent ones. The American Red Cross, the National Academy of Sciences and the National Research Council are Offices of this sort. A quasi-official government agency is one which is only partially under the federal government. The National Academy of Sciences was founded by Congress in 1863. Its main purpose is to investigate and report on any subject of art or science requested by the government. Money for specific reports can be appropriated by Congress, but the Academy itself receives no federal funds whatsoever for services rendered to the government. The National Research Council was set up under the National Academy of Sciences by request of President Woodrow Wilson in 1916. National preparedness was and still is the subject of its research, but, like the Academy, it receives no federal funds. The American Red Cross, which was created in 1905 by Act of Congress, has national headquarters in Washington and works closely with the government in assisting in any national disaster. Its work is carried out almost entirely by volunteers and is paid for entirely by voluntary contributions. Its purpose is to help the sick, or needy, in hospitals, at home or in disaster stricken areas. It also exists to provide volunteer aid in time of war to the wounded or sick and to act as a means of communication between the members of the Armed Forces and the people of the United States. The Red Cross operates across the nation and cooperates with all government and private agencies in assisting those who need its help. It also is a part of the International Red Cross whose headquarters are in Switzerland.

This abbreviated list of the independent and quasi-official agencies of the government makes clear the many fields in which the federal government has an interest at the present time. They also serve as another example of the ability of the government to delegate responsibility and to cover many fields necessary to the benefit of the people in an organized and efficient way. Had the government stood still and been unable to expand, the problems arising in a growing nation could never have been handled, and the system would have collapsed under the burdens and necessities of the twentieth century.

The Federal Government and the Citizen

This book is only a brief and by no means complete discussion of some of the many parts of the United States government. It is extraordinary to think that the Constitution whose Preamble is only one sentence and whose body is but a few pages could be the foundation of the enormous and complicated structure that is the nation's government today. The size of the government may be overwhelming and seem far removed from the short outline of the Constitution, but its increase in size has not meant that the government has veered from the purpose stated in the Preamble. To realize the phrase "in order to form a more perfect union" has been the purpose of each addition to the federal government. As life has grown more complicated with new economic, social, scientific and international developments, there has been repeatedly the need to increase the responsibilities and duties of the federal government. A backward glance over the years that the government of the United States has been in existence proves that the government has met the challenge of new situations often by adding a department, an agency or even a bureau in order to accept the new responsibility. Also the constant reorganizations of sections of the government have been attempts to make the government a good servant of the people and one equipped to handle its diversified responsibilities.

To realize the fundamental belief that the purpose of government is to serve the people in all ways, the United States government has entered into the lives of every American today to a great extent although we may not be aware of it. Much that we take for granted today is only available and possible for us because of the activities of the many branches of the federal government. Two widely varied examples will serve to prove this statement.

Orange juice is the most common of breakfast items. How can this everyday beverage reflect the interest and the workings of the United States government? Before that orange arrives on the breakfast table many departments of the federal government have had something to do with it. First, the housewife at the market before she buys the fruit can choose between several grades of oranges each for a different price. Why? The Congress of the United States has passed legislation requiring the grading of fruit according to size and color; the price is fixed accordingly, the larger the orange, the higher the price. Naturally the orange grower wants to produce the best product in order to get more profit. How can he grow the best fruit? He can go to the United States Department of Agriculture. Agricultural Research Centers are largely responsible for the development of fertilizers, sprays and methods of grafting trees which all result in the growing of better fruit. Other divisions of the department provide on the spot help to the farmer in planning his grove or in providing machinery, perhaps for spraying. The United States Weather Bureau also contributes to the growing of the orange. Advance warnings of frost will help the farmer. He puts smudge pots in the groves in order to keep his trees from being frostbitten. Once the orange is grown and harvested, the United States Department of Agriculture inspectors grade the fruit, attesting to its size and color. Marketing services also provided by the Agricultural Department can help the grower to sell his fruit to the best advantage. Once the grower has sold his fruit to a wholesaler, it must travel to markets all over the country. At this point the Interstate Commerce Commission enters into the picture. Because the fruit must cross State borders, the trucking and railroad industries are regulated by the federal government. Rates, health and sanitation codes, refrigeration temperatures are all standardized for the protection of the transport companies and for the consumers who buy the fruit at the local markets. When the fruit is unpacked at its destination and the retail price affixed, inspectors check to see that price and quality correspond correctly. By the time the orange is in the consumer's kitchen, it has been almost constantly under the surveillance of the United States government. Because of this government interest, the orange is all it should be and the person who drinks its juice does so casually and in complete confidence that the fruit is pure and wholesome, probably never thinking of the many federal government employees whose labors brought that orange to his table.

Another example of the workings of many government departments for the benefit of the American people is in the commercial shipping business. Every American merchant ship that sets sail for foreign ports does so in the first place because of the State Department's arrangements. Ships cannot sail freely in and out of ports around the world. Commercial treaties must be made between nations. These treaties are made by the State Department. Once the treaty is made, the first step toward the ship's sailing is taken, but before it can actually leave port, other government departments have work to do. The ship, which may have been constructed partly with government funds, must be inspected by the Bureau of Customs for safety and for assessment of tonnage duties. The crew must be checked both by the Public Health Service and by Internal Security agents. The Bureau of Narcotics and Dangerous Drugs of the Department of Justice also checks the ship and the men for possible infringement of the narcotics' laws. When the ship receives clearance from these government officials, it may sail. As it sails, however, it is under the protection of the United States Coast Guard which is not only prepared to effect a sea rescue in case of disaster, but also has cleared the shipping lanes of hazards and icebergs if in the north. The United States Weather Bureau supplies the latest forecasts, important for the safety of the ship. Should the ship sail in coastal waters, the necessary charts are obtained from the Environmental Science Services Administrator in the Department of Commerce. Once the ship is abroad, the State Department reenters the picture. The American seamen are under the protection of the United States Consulates in foreign ports. Any information that they should require or any protection of their rights as American citizens is given by the American Foreign Service abroad. Although the ship may be far from the United States, the federal government is as concerned with it and its crew as though it were at dock in New York City.

These are but two examples of the way in which the United States government affects the life and business of Americans. There are many more obvious ways also in which we are made aware of the federal government. Few do not know of the scientific experiments made by the Armed Forces. Legislative programs of Congress are reported daily in the press. Supreme Court decisions are always handed down on Mondays and are published in the newspapers Monday evenings and Tuesday mornings. Hardly a day goes by without the President's activities and ideas being relayed to the nation. No one can really spend a day without being aware in some way or another of the United States government.

When the extent, as well as the necessity, of the United States government's activities are known and understood, it then becomes apparent that to support this government is the responsibility of every citizen. The great size of the government explains the need for many taxes. Every government employee must be paid; every government building must be maintained; new buildings must be built; and every government program must be carried out both domestically and abroad. Money is fundamental to the success of the government, and the cost must be met. Tax money pays the bills. Without the money collected in revenue, it would be impossible to have a government. Instead of a country whose citizens are the most prosperous, the best fed and have the best possible health facilities, there would be a weak and disorganized country without the power to stand up for freedom against tyranny. Though taxes are unpleasant to pay, it is the duty of every citizen to share the cost of the benefits which he receives from the federal government.

The citizen is not only called upon to pay his share of the taxes, but he is also responsible for another and equally important contribution to his government. That is interest in it. Democratic government can only succeed if the citizenry is willing to take the responsibility of being interested in the problems of government and in voting. The United States federal government is made up essentially of elected representatives of the people. Those who are appointed to important executive positions are chosen by the President who is elected and they must be confirmed by the elected representatives of the people in Congress, the Senators. If the people of the United States are not interested in voting and taking democratic responsibility, they will pay the consequences. They will have to accept men in government whom they have not chosen. An alert and interested electorate is the greatest safeguard of liberty. The Constitution so ordered the federal government that the people have the greatest power. If they refuse to accept this great responsibility, they will no longer have democracy. If they choose to exercise their privileges as one of the freest people on earth, they will, in turn, maintain good and honest government, truly dedicated to serving the best interests of the electorate. The responsibility and importance of the voters have increased perhaps with the growth of the federal government. Such an enormous operation covering so many different fields of activity with so many thousands of employees can give rise to corruption. The only way to avoid dishonesty in government and to safeguard the people's interests is by constant vigilance. An enlightened, intelligent and interested voting public is the first step in the practice of vigilance. Expensive as it is, complicated as its duties are, the United States form of constitutional government has proven since the day of its founding its worth in its service to the people of this nation. It shall continue to serve Americans as long as they are willing to deserve it.

The Constitution
of the
United States of America

WE THE PEOPLE of the United States, in Order to form a more perfect Union, establish Justice, insure domestic Tranquility, provide for the common defence, promote the general Welfare, and secure the Blessings of Liberty to ourselves and our Posterity, do ordain and establish this Constitution for the United States of America.

ARTICLE. I.

SECTION. 1. All legislative Powers herein granted shall be vested in a Congress of the United States, which shall consist of a Senate and House of Representatives.

SECTION. 2. The House of Representatives shall be composed of Members chosen every second Year by the People of the several States, and the Electors in each State shall have the Qualifications requisite for Electors of the most numerous Branch of the State Legislature.

No person shall be a Representative who shall not have attained to the Age of twenty five Years, and been seven Years a Citizen of the United States, and who shall not, when elected, be an Inhabitant of that State in which he shall be chosen.

[Representatives and direct Taxes shall be apportioned among the several States which may be included within this Union, according to their respective Numbers, which shall be determined by adding to the whole Number of free Persons, including those bound to Service for a Term of Years, and excluding Indians not taxed, three fifths of all other Persons]. The actual Enumeration shall be made within three Years after the first Meeting of the Congress of the United States, and within every subsequent Term of ten Years, in such Manner as they shall by Law direct. The Number of Representatives shall not exceed one for every thirty Thousand, but each State shall have at Least one Representative; and until such enumeration shall be made, the State of New Hampshire shall be entitled to chuse three, Massachusetts eight, Rhode-Island and Providence Plantations one, Connecticut five, New-York six, New Jersey four, Pennsylvania eight, Delaware one, Maryland six, Virginia ten, North Carolina five, South Carolina five, and Georgia three.

When vacancies happen in the Representation from any State, the Executive Authority thereof shall issue Writs of Election to fill such Vacancies.

The House of Representatives shall chuse their Speaker and other Officers; and shall have the sole Power of Impeachment.

SECTION. 3. The Senate of the United States shall be composed of two Senators from each State, [chosen by the Legislature thereof,] for six Years; and each Senator shall have one Vote.

Immediately after they shall be assembled in Consequence of the first Election, they shall be divided as equally as may be into three Classes. The Seats of the Senators of the first Class shall be vacated at the Expiration of the second Year, of the second Class at the Expiration of the fourth Year, and of the third Class at the Expiration of the sixth Year, so that one third may be chosen every second Year; [and if Vacancies happen by Resignation, or otherwise, during the Recess of the Legislature of any State, the Executive thereof may make temporary Appointments until the next Meeting of the Legislature, which shall then fill such Vacancies].

No Person shall be a Senator who shall not have attained to the Age of thirty Years, and been nine Years a Citizen of the United States, and who shall not, when elected, be an Inhabitant of that State for which he shall be chosen.

The Vice President of the United States shall be President of the Senate, but shall have no Vote, unless they be equally divided.

The Senate shall chuse their other Officers, and also a President pro tempore, in the Absence of the Vice President, or when he shall exercise the Office of President of the United States.

The Senate shall have the sole Power to try all Impeachments. When sitting for that Purpose, they shall be on Oath or Affirmation. When the President of the United States is tried, the Chief Justice shall preside: And no Person shall be convicted without the Concurrence of two thirds of the Members present.

Judgment in Cases of Impeachment shall not extend further than to removal from Office, and disqualification to hold and enjoy any Office of honor, Trust or Profit under the United States: but the Party convicted shall nevertheless be liable and subject to Indictment, Trial, Judgment and Punishment, according to Law.

SECTION. 4. The Times, Places and Manner of holding Elections for Senators and Representatives, shall be prescribed in each State by the Legislature thereof; but the Congress may at any time by Law make or alter such Regulations, except as to the Places of chusing Senators.

The Congress shall assemble at least once in every Year, and such Meeting shall [be on the first Monday in December,] unless they shall by Law appoint a different Day.

SECTION. 5. Each House shall be the Judge of the Elections, Returns and Qualifications of its own Members, and a Majority of each shall constitute a Quorum to do Business; but a smaller Number may adjourn from day to day, and may be authorized to compel the Attendance of absent Members, in such Manner, and under such Penalties as each House may provide.

Each House may determine the Rules of its Proceedings, punish its Members for disorderly Behaviour, and, with the Concurrence of two thirds, expel a Member.

Each House shall keep a Journal of its Proceedings, and from time to time publish the same, excepting such Parts as may in their Judgment require Secrecy; and the Yeas and Nays of the Members of either House on any question shall, at the Desire of one fifth of those Present, be entered on the Journal.

Neither House, during the Session of Congress, shall, without the Consent of the other, adjourn for more than three days, nor to any other Place than that in which the two Houses shall be sitting.

Section. 6. The Senators and Representatives shall receive a Compensation for their Services, to be ascertained by Law, and paid out of the Treasury of the United States. They shall in all Cases, except Treason, Felony and Breach of the Peace, be privileged from Arrest during their Attendance at the Session of their respective Houses, and in going to and returning from the same; and for any Speech or Debate in either House, they shall not be questioned in any other Place.

No Senator or Representative shall, during the Time for which he was elected, be appointed to any civil Office under the Authority of the United States, which shall have been created, or the Emoluments whereof shall have been encreased during such time; and no Person holding any Office under the United States, shall be a Member of either House during his Continuance in Office.

Section. 7. All Bills for raising Revenue shall originate in the House of Representatives; but the Senate may propose or concur with Amendments as on other Bills.

Every Bill which shall have passed the House of Representatives and the Senate, shall, before it become a Law, be presented to the President of the United States; If he approve he shall sign it, but if not he shall return it, with his Objections to that House in which it shall have originated, who shall enter the Objections at large on their Journal, and proceed to reconsider it. If after such Reconsideration two thirds of that House shall agree to pass the Bill, it shall be sent, together with the Objections, to the other House, by which it shall likewise be reconsidered, and if approved by two thirds of that House, it shall become a Law. But in all such Cases the Votes of both Houses shall be determined by yeas and Nays, and the Names of the Persons voting for and against the Bill shall be entered on the Journal of each House respectively. If any Bill shall not be returned by the President within ten Days (Sundays excepted) after it shall have been presented to him, the Same shall be a Law, in like Manner as if he had signed it, unless the Congress by their Adjournment prevent its Return, in which Case it shall not be a Law.

Every Order, Resolution, or Vote to which the Concurrence of the Senate and House of Representatives may be necessary (except on a question of Adjournment) shall be presented to the President of the United States; and before the Same shall take Effect, shall be approved by him, or being disapproved by him, shall be repassed by two thirds of the Senate and House of Representatives, according to the Rules and Limitations prescribed in the Case of a Bill.

Section. 8. The Congress shall have Power To lay and collect Taxes, Duties, Imposts and Excises, to pay the Debts and provide for the common Defence and general Welfare of the United States; but all Duties, Imposts and Excises shall be uniform throughout the United States;

To borrow Money on the credit of the United States;

To regulate Commerce with foreign Nations, and among the several States, and with the Indian Tribes;

To establish an uniform Rule of Naturalization, and uniform Laws on the subject of Bankruptcies throughout the United States;

To coin Money, regulate the Value thereof, and of foreign Coin, and fix the Standard of Weights and Measures;

To provide for the Punishment of counterfeiting the Securities and current Coin of the United States;

To establish Post Offices and post Roads;

To promote the Progress of Science and useful Arts, by securing for limited Times to Authors and Inventors the exclusive Right to their respective Writings and Discoveries;

To constitute Tribunals inferior to the supreme Court;

To define and punish Piracies and Felonies committed on the high Seas, and Offences against the Law of Nations;

To declare War, grant Letters of Marque and Reprisal, and make Rules concerning Captures on Land and Water;

To raise and support Armies, but no Appropriation of Money to that Use shall be for a longer Term than two Years;

To provide and maintain a Navy;

To make Rules for the Government and Regulation of the land and naval Forces;

To provide for calling forth the Militia to execute the Laws of the Union, suppress Insurrections and repel Invasions;

To provide for organizing, arming, and disciplining, the Militia, and for governing such Part of them as may be employed in the Service of the United States, reserving to the States respectively, the Appointment of the Officers, and the Authority of training the Militia according to the discipline prescribed by Congress;

To exercise exclusive Legislation in all Cases whatsoever, over such District (not exceeding ten Miles square) as may, by Cession of particular States, and the Acceptance of Congress, become the Seat of the Government of the United States, and to exercise like Authority over all Places purchased by the Consent of the Legislature of the State in which the Same shall be, for the Erection of Forts, Magazines, Arsenals, dock-Yards, and other needful Buildings;—And

To make all Laws which shall be necessary and proper for carrying into Execution the foregoing Powers, and all other Powers vested by this Constitution in the Government of the United States, or in any Department or Officer thereof.

Section. 9. The Migration or Importation of such Persons as any of the States now existing shall think proper to admit, shall not be prohibited by the Congress prior to the Year one thousand eight hundred and eight, but a Tax or duty may be imposed on such Importation, not exceeding ten dollars for each Person.

The Privilege of the Writ of Habeas Corpus shall not be suspended, unless when in Cases of Rebellion or Invasion the public Safety may require it.

No Bill of Attainder or ex post facto Law shall be passed.

No Capitation, or other direct, Tax shall be laid, unless in Proportion to the Census or Enumeration herein before directed to be taken.

No Tax or Duty shall be laid on Articles exported from any State.

No Preference shall be given by any Regulation of Commerce or Revenue to the Ports of one State over those of another: nor shall Vessels bound to, or from, one State, be obliged to enter, clear, or pay Duties in another.

No Money shall be drawn from the Treasury, but in Consequence of Appropriations made by Law; and a regular Statement and Account of the Receipts and Expenditures of all public Money shall be published from time to time.

No Title of Nobility shall be granted by the United States: And no Person holding any Office of Profit or Trust under them, shall, without the Consent of the Congress, accept of any present, Emolument, Office, or Title, of any kind whatever, from any King, Prince, or foreign State.

SECTION. 10. No State shall enter into any Treaty, Alliance, or Confederation; grant Letters of Marque and Reprisal; coin Money; emit Bills of Credit; make any Thing but gold and silver Coin a Tender in Payment of Debts; pass any Bill of Attainder, ex post facto Law, or Law impairing the Obligation of Contracts, or grant any Title of Nobility.

No State shall, without the Consent of the Congress, lay any Imposts or Duties on Imports or Exports, except what may be absolutely necessary for executing it's inspection Laws: and the net Produce of all Duties and Imposts, laid by any State on Imports or Exports, shall be for the Use of the Treasury of the United States; and all such Laws shall be subject to the Revision and Controul of the Congress.

No State shall, without the Consent of Congress, lay any Duty of Tonnage, keep Troops, or Ships of War in time of Peace, enter into any Agreement or Compact with another State, or with a foreign Power, or engage in War, unless actually invaded, or in such imminent Danger as will not admit of delay.

ARTICLE. II.

SECTION. 1. The executive Power shall be vested in a President of the United States of America. He shall hold his Office during the Term of four Years, and together with the Vice President, chosen for the same Term, be elected, as follows

Each State shall appoint, in such Manner as the Legislature thereof may direct, a Number of Electors, equal to the whole Number of Senators and Representatives to which the State may be entitled in the Congress: but no Senator or Representative, or Person holding an Office of Trust or Profit under the United States, shall be appointed an Elector.

[The Electors shall meet in their respective States, and vote by Ballot for two Persons, of whom one at least shall not be an Inhabitant of the same State with themselves. And they shall make a List of all the Persons voted for, and of the Number of Votes for each; which List they shall sign and certify, and transmit sealed to the Seat of the Government of the United States, directed to the President of the Senate. The President of the Senate shall, in the Presence of the Senate and House of Representatives, open all the Certificates, and the Votes shall then be counted. The Person having the greatest Number of Votes shall be the President, if such Number be a Majority of the whole Number of Electors appointed; and if there be more than one who have such Majority, and have an equal Number of Votes, then the House of Representatives shall immediately chuse by Ballot one of them for President; and if no Person have a Majority, then from the five highest on the List the said House shall in like Manner chuse the President. But in chusing the President, the Votes shall be taken by States, the Representation from each State having one Vote; A quorum for this Purpose shall consist of a Member or Members from two thirds of the States, and a Majority of all the States shall be necessary to a Choice. In every Case, after the Choice of the President, the Person having the greatest Number of Votes of the Electors shall be the Vice President. But if there should remain two or more who have equal Votes, the Senate shall chuse from them by Ballot the Vice President.]

The Congress may determine the Time of chusing the Electors, and the Day on which they shall give their Votes; which Day shall be the same throughout the United States.

No Person except a natural born Citizen, or a Citizen of the United States, at the time of the Adoption of this Constitution, shall be eligible to the Office of President; neither shall any Person be eligible to that Office who shall not have attained to the Age of thirty five Years, and been fourteen Years a Resident within the United States.

In Case of the Removal of the President from Office, or of his Death, Resignation, or Inability to discharge the Powers and Duties of the said Office, the Same shall devolve on the Vice President, and the Congress may by Law provide for the Case of Removal, Death, Resignation or Inability, both of the President and Vice President, declaring what Officer shall then act as President, and such Officer shall act accordingly, until the Disability be removed, or a President shall be elected.

The President shall, at stated Times, receive for his Services, a Compensation, which shall neither be encreased nor diminished during the Period for which he shall have been elected, and he shall not receive within that Period any other Emolument from the United States, or any of them.

Before he enter on the Execution of his Office, he shall take the following Oath or Affirmation:—"I do solemnly swear (or affirm) that I will faithfully execute the Office of President of the United States, and will to the best of my Ability, preserve, protect and defend the Constitution of the United States."

SECTION. 2. The President shall be Commander in Chief of the Army and Navy of the United States, and of the Militia of the several States, when called into the actual Service of the United States; he may require the Opinion, in writing, of the principal Officer in each of the executive Departments, upon any Subject relating to the Duties of their respective Offices, and he shall have Power to grant Reprieves and Pardons for Offences against the United States, except in Cases of Impeachment.

He shall have Power, by and with the Advice and Consent of the Senate, to make Treaties, provided two thirds of the Senators present concur; and he shall nominate, and by and with the Advice and Consent of the Senate, shall appoint Ambassadors, other public Ministers and Consuls, Judges of the supreme Court, and all other Officers of the United States, whose Appointments are not herein otherwise provided for, and which shall be established by Law: but the Congress may by Law vest the Appointment of such inferior Officers, as they think proper, in the President alone, in the Courts of Law, or in the Heads of Departments.

The President shall have Power to fill up all Vacancies that may happen during the Recess of the Senate, by granting Commissions which shall expire at the End of their next Session.

SECTION. 3. He shall from time to time give to the Congress Information of the State of the Union, and recommend to their Consideration such Measures as he shall judge necessary and expedient; he may, on extraordinary Occasions, convene both Houses, or either of them, and in Case of Disagreement between them, with

Respect of the Time of Adjournment, he may adjourn them to such Time as he shall think proper; he shall receive Ambassadors and other public Ministers; he shall take Care that the Laws be faithfully executed, and shall Commission all the Officers of the United States.

SECTION. 4. The President, Vice President and all civil Officers of the United States, shall be removed from Office on Impeachment for, and Conviction of, Treason, Bribery, or other high Crimes and Misdemeanors.

ARTICLE. III.

SECTION. 1. The judicial Power of the United States, shall be vested in one supreme Court, and in such inferior Courts as the Congress may from time to time ordain and establish. The Judges, both of the supreme and inferior Courts, shall hold their Offices during good Behaviour, and shall, at stated Times, receive for their Services, a Compensation, which shall not be diminished during their Continuance in Office.

SECTION. 2. The judicial Power shall extend to all Cases, in Law and Equity, arising under this Constitution, the Laws of the United States, and Treaties made, or which shall be made, under their Authority;—to all Cases affecting Ambassadors, other public Ministers and Consuls;—to all Cases of admiralty and maritime Jurisdiction;—to Controversies to which the United States shall be a Party;—to Controversies between two or more States;—between a State and Citizens of another State;—between Citizens of different States,—between Citizens of the same State claiming Lands under Grants of different States, and between a State, or the Citizens thereof, and foreign States, Citizens or Subjects.

In all Cases affecting Ambassadors, other public Ministers and Consuls, and those in which a State shall be Party, the supreme Court shall have original Jurisdiction. In all the other Cases before mentioned, the supreme Court shall have appellate Jurisdiction, both as to Law and Fact, with such Exceptions, and under such Regulations as the Congress shall make.

The Trial of all Crimes, except in Cases of Impeachment, shall be by Jury; and such Trial shall be held in the State where the said Crimes shall have been committed; but when not committed within any State, the Trial shall be at such Place or Places as the Congress may by Law have directed.

SECTION. 3. Treason against the United States, shall consist only in levying War against them, or in adhering to their Enemies, giving them Aid and Comfort. No Person shall be convicted of Treason unless on the Testimony of two Witnesses to the same overt Act, or on Confession in open Court.

The Congress shall have Power to declare the Punishment of Treason, but no Attainder of Treason shall work Corruption of Blood, or Forfeiture except during the Life of the Person attainted.

ARTICLE. IV.

SECTION. 1. Full Faith and Credit shall be given in each State to the public Acts, Records, and judicial Proceedings of every other State. And the Congress may by general Laws prescribe the Manner in which such Acts, Records and Proceedings shall be proved, and the Effect thereof.

SECTION. 2. The Citizens of each State shall be entitled to all Privileges and Immunities of Citizens in the several States.

A Person charged in any State with Treason, Felony, or other Crime, who shall flee from Justice, and be found in another State, shall on Demand of the executive Authority of the State from which he fled, be delivered up, to be removed to the State having Jurisdiction of the Crime.

[No Person held to Service or Labour in one State, under the Laws thereof, escaping into another, shall, in Consequence of any Law or Regulation therein, be discharged from such Service or Labour, but shall be delivered up on Claim of the Party to whom such Service or Labour may be due.]

SECTION. 3. New States may be admitted by the Congress into this Union; but no new State shall be formed or erected within the Jurisdiction of any other State; nor any State be formed by the Junction of two or more States, or Parts of States, without the Consent of the Legislatures of the States concerned as well as of the Congress.

The Congress shall have Power to dispose of and make all needful Rules and Regulations respecting the Territory or other Property belonging to the United States; and nothing in this Constitution shall be so construed as to Prejudice any Claims of the United States, or of any particular State.

SECTION. 4. The United States shall guarantee to every State in this Union a Republican Form of Government, and shall protect each of them against Invasion; and on Application of the Legislature, or of the Executive (when the Legislature cannot be convened) against domestic Violence.

ARTICLE. V.

The Congress, whenever two thirds of both Houses shall deem it necessary, shall propose Amendments to this Constitution, or, on the Application of the Legislatures of two thirds of the several States, shall call a Convention for proposing Amendments, which, in either Case, shall be valid to all Intents and Purposes, as Part of this Constitution, when ratified by the Legislatures of three fourths of the several States, or by Conventions in three fourths thereof, as the one or the other Mode of Ratification may be proposed by the Congress; Provided [that no Amendment which may be made prior to the Year One thousand eight hundred and eight shall in any Manner affect the first and fourth Clauses in the Ninth Section of the first Article; and] that no State, without its Consent, shall be deprived of its equal Suffrage in the Senate.

ARTICLE. VI.

All Debts contracted and Engagements entered into, before the Adoption of this Constitution, shall be as valid against the United States under this Constitution, as under the Confederation.

This Constitution, and the Laws of the United States which shall be made in Pursuance thereof; and all Treaties made, or which shall be made, under the Authority of the United States, shall be the supreme Law of the Land; and the Judges in every State shall be bound thereby, any Thing in the Constitution or Laws of any State to the Contrary notwithstanding.

The Senators and Representatives before mentioned, and the Members of the several State Legislatures, and all executive and judicial Officers, both of the United States and of the several States, shall be bound by Oath or Affirmation, to support this Constitution; but no religious Test shall ever be required as a Qualification to any Office or public Trust under the United States.

CONSTITUTION OF THE UNITED STATES

ARTICLE. VII.

The Ratification of the Conventions of nine States, shall be sufficient for the Establishment of this Constitution between the States so ratifying the Same.

DONE in Convention by the Unanimous Consent of the States present the Seventeenth Day of September in the Year of our Lord one thousand seven hundred and Eighty seven and of the Independence of the United States of America the Twelfth IN WITNESS whereof We have hereunto subscribed our Names,

Go WASHINGTON—
Presid^t. *and deputy from Virginia.*

New Hampshire.

JOHN LANGDON,	NICHOLAS GILMAN.

Massachusetts.

NATHANIEL GORHAM,	RUFUS KING.

Connecticut.

WM. SAML. JOHNSON,	ROGER SHERMAN.

New York.

ALEXANDER HAMILTON.

New Jersey.

WIL: LIVINGSTON,	WM. PATERSON,
DAVID BREARLEY,	JONA: DAYTON.

Pennsylvania.

B FRANKLIN,	THOMAS MIFFLIN,
ROB^T MORRIS,	GEO. CLYMER,
THOS. FITZSIMONS,	JARED INGERSOLL,
JAMES WILSON,	GOUV MORRIS.

Delaware.

GEO: READ,	GUNNING BEDFORD, jun,
JOHN DICKINSON,	RICHARD BASSETT.
JACO: BROOM,	

Maryland.

JAMES MCHENRY,	DAN OF S^T THOS. JENIFER,
DAN^L CARROLL.	

Virginia.

JOHN BLAIR—	JAMES MADISON JR.

North Carolina.

WM. BLOUNT,	RICH'D DOBBS SPAIGHT,
HU WILLIAMSON.	

South Carolina.

J. RUTLEDGE   CHARLES COTESWORTH PINCKNEY,
CHARLES PINCKNEY,   PIERCE BUTLER.

Georgia.

WILLIAM FEW,   ABR BALDWIN.
    Attest: WILLIAM JACKSON, *Secretary.*

The text of the Constitution, as given above, is from the engrossed copy signed by thirty-nine framers, which is now enshrined in the National Archives and Records Service, General Services Administration, Washington, D.C. The official records relating to the Amendments, which follow, are also permanently located in the National Archives.

The parts included in brackets have since been changed because of amendments or obsolescence.

AMENDMENTS

The first ten Amendments were ratified December 15, 1791, and form what is known as the Bill of Rights

ARTICLES IN ADDITION TO, AND AMENDMENT OF, THE CONSTITUTION OF THE UNITED STATES OF AMERICA, PROPOSED BY CONGRESS, AND RATIFIED BY THE LEGISLATURES OF THE SEVERAL STATES PURSUANT TO THE FIFTH ARTICLE OF THE ORIGINAL CONSTITUTION

ARTICLE [I]*

Congress shall make no law respecting an establishment of religion, or prohibiting the free exercise thereof; or abridging the freedom of speech, or of the press; or the right of the people peaceably to assemble, and to petition the Government for a redress of grievances.

ARTICLE [II]

A well regulated Militia, being necessary to the security of a free State, the right of the people to keep and bear Arms, shall not be infringed.

ARTICLE [III]

No Soldier shall, in time of peace be quartered in any house, without the consent of the Owner, nor in time of war, but in a manner to be prescribed by law.

ARTICLE [IV]

The right of the people to be secure in their persons, houses, papers, and effects, against unreasonable searches and seizures, shall not be violated, and no Warrants shall issue, but upon probable cause, supported by Oath or affirmation, and particularly describing the place to be searched, and the persons or things to be seized.

*Only the 13th, 14th, 15th, and 16th articles of amendment had numbers assigned to them at the time of ratification.

ARTICLE [V]

No person shall be held to answer for a capital, or otherwise infamous crime, unless on a presentment or indictment of a Grand Jury, except in cases arising in the land or naval forces, or in the Militia, when in actual service in time of War or public danger; nor shall any person be subject for the same offence to be twice put in jeopardy of life or limb; nor shall be compelled in any criminal case to be a witness against himself, nor be deprived of life, liberty, or property, without due process of law; nor shall private property be taken for public use without just compensation.

ARTICLE [VI]

In all criminal prosecutions, the accused shall enjoy the right to a speedy and public trial, by an impartial jury of the State and district wherein the crime shall have been committed, which district shall have been previously ascertained by law, and to be informed of the nature and cause of the accusation; to be confronted with the witnesses against him; to have compulsory process for obtaining Witnesses in his favor, and to have the assistance of counsel for his defence.

ARTICLE [VII]

In Suits at common law, where the value in controversy shall exceed twenty dollars, the right of trial by jury shall be preserved, and no fact tried by a jury, shall be otherwise reexamined in any Court of the United States, than according to the rules of the common law.

ARTICLE [VIII]

Excessive bail shall not be required, nor excessive fines imposed, nor cruel and unusual punishments inflicted.

ARTICLE [IX]

The enumeration in the Constitution, of certain rights, shall not be construed to deny or disparage others retained by the people.

ARTICLE [X]

The powers not delegated to the United States by the Constitution, nor prohibited by it to the States, are reserved to the States respectively, or to the people.

ARTICLE [XI]

The Judicial power of the United States shall not be construed to extend to any suit in law or equity, commenced or prosecuted against one of the United States by Citizens of another State, or by Citizens or Subjects of any Foreign State.

ARTICLE [XII]

The electors shall meet in their respective states and vote by ballot for President and Vice-President, one of whom, at least, shall not be an inhabitant of the same state with themselves; they shall name in their ballots the person voted for as President, and in distinct ballots the person voted for as Vice-President, and they shall make distinct lists of all persons voted for as President, and of all persons voted for as Vice-President, and of the number of votes for each, which lists they shall sign and certify, and transmit sealed to the seat of the government of the United States, directed to the President of the Senate;—The President of the Senate shall, in the presence of the Senate and House of Representatives, open all the certificates and the votes shall then be counted;—The person having the greatest number of votes for President, shall be the President, if such number be a majority of the whole number of Electors appointed; and if no person have such majority, then from the persons having the highest numbers not exceeding three on the list of those voted for as President, the House of Representatives shall choose immediately, by ballot, the President. But in choosing the President, the votes shall be taken by states, the representation from each state having one vote; a quorum for this purpose shall consist of a member or members from two-thirds of the states, and a majority of all the states shall be necessary to a choice. [And if the House of Representatives shall not choose a President whenever the right of choice shall devolve upon them, before the fourth day of March next following, then the Vice-President shall act as President, as in the case of the death or other constitutional disability of the President.] The person having the greatest number of votes as Vice-President, shall be the Vice-President, if such number be a majority of the whole number of Electors appointed, and if no person have a majority, then from the two highest numbers on the list, the Senate shall choose the Vice-President; a quorum for the purpose shall consist of two-thirds of the whole number of Senators, and a majority of the whole number shall be necessary to a choice. But no person constitutionally ineligible to the office of President shall be eligible to that of Vice-President of the United States.

ARTICLE XIII

SECTION 1. Neither slavery nor involuntary servitude, except as a punishment for crime whereof the party shall have been duly convicted, shall exist within the United States, or any place subject to their jurisdiction.

SECTION 2. Congress shall have power to enforce this article by appropriate legislation.

ARTICLE XIV

SECTION 1. All persons born or naturalized in the United States, and subject to the jurisdiction thereof, are citizens of the United States and of the State wherein they reside. No State shall make or enforce any law which shall abridge the privileges or immunities of citizens of the United States; nor shall any State deprive any person of life, liberty, or property, without due process of law; nor deny to any person within its jurisdiction the equal protection of the laws.

SECTION 2. Representatives shall be apportioned among the several States according to their respective numbers, counting the whole number of persons in each State, excluding Indians not taxed. But when the right to vote at any election for the choice of electors for President and Vice President of the United States, Representatives in Congress, the Executive and Judicial officers of a State, or the members of the Legislature thereof, is denied to any of the male inhabitants of such State, being twenty-one years of age, and citizens of the United States, or in any way abridged, except for participation in rebellion, or other crime, the basis of representation therein shall be reduced in the proportion which the number of such male citizens shall bear to the whole number of male citizens twenty-one years of age in such State.

SECTION 3. No person shall be a Senator or Representative in Congress, or elector of President and Vice President, or hold any office, civil or military, under the United States, or under any State, who, having previously taken an oath, as a member of Congress, or as an officer of the United States, or as a member of any State legislature, or as an executive or judicial officer of any State, to support the Constitution of the United States, shall have engaged in insurrection or rebellion against the same, or given aid or comfort to the enemies thereof. But Congress may by a vote of two-thirds of each House, remove such disability.

SECTION 4. The validity of the public debt of the United States, authorized by law, including debts incurred for payment of pensions and bounties for services in suppressing insurrection or rebellion, shall not be questioned. But neither the United States nor any State shall assume or pay any debt or obligation incurred in aid of insurrection or rebellion against the United States, or any claim for the loss or emancipation of any slave; but all such debts, obligations and claims shall be held illegal and void.

SECTION 5. The Congress shall have power to enforce, by appropriate legislation, the provisions of this article.

ARTICLE XV

SECTION 1. The right of citizens of the United States to vote shall not be denied or abridged by the United States or by any State on account of race, color, or previous condition of servitude.

SECTION 2. The Congress shall have power to enforce this article by appropriate legislation.

ARTICLE XVI

The Congress shall have power to lay and collect taxes on incomes, from whatever source derived, without apportionment among the several States, and without regard to any census or enumeration.

ARTICLE [XVII]

The Senate of the United States shall be composed of two Senators from each State, elected by the people thereof, for six years; and each Senator shall have one vote. The electors in each State shall have the qualifications requisite for electors of the most numerous branch of the State legislatures.

When vacancies happen in the representation of any State in the Senate, the executive authority of such State shall issue writs of election to fill such vacancies: *Provided*, That the legislature of any State may empower the executive thereof to make temporary appointments until the people fill the vacancies by election as the legislature may direct.

This amendment shall not be so construed as to affect the election or term of any Senator chosen before it becomes valid as part of the Constitution.

[ARTICLE [XVIII]

[SECTION 1. After one year from the ratification of this article the manufacture. sale, or transportation of intoxicating liquors within, the importation thereof into, or the exportation thereof from the United States and all territory subject to the jurisdiction thereof for beverage purposes is hereby prohibited.

[Section 2. The Congress and the several States shall have concurrent power to enforce this article by appropriate legislation.

[Section 3. This article shall be inoperative unless it shall have been ratified as an amendment to the Constitution by the legislatures of the several States, as provided in the Constitution, within seven years from the date of the submission hereof to the States by the Congress.]

ARTICLE [XIX]

The right of citizens of the United States to vote shall not be denied or abridged by the United States or by any State on account of sex.

Congress shall have power to enforce this article by appropriate legislation.

ARTICLE [XX]

Section 1. The terms of the President and Vice President shall end at noon on the 20th day of January, and the terms of Senators and Representatives at noon on the 3d day of January, of the years in which such terms would have ended if this article had not been ratified; and the terms of their successors shall then begin.

Section 2. The Congress shall assemble at least once in every year, and such meeting shall begin at noon on the 3d day of January, unless they shall by law appoint a different day.

Section 3. If, at the time fixed for the beginning of the term of the President, the President elect shall have died, the Vice President elect shall become President. If a President shall not have been chosen before the time fixed for the beginning of his term, or if the President elect shall have failed to qualify, then the Vice President elect shall act as President until a President shall have qualified; and the Congress may by law provide for the case wherein neither a President elect nor a Vice President elect shall have qualified, declaring who shall then act as President, or the manner in which one who is to act shall be selected, and such person shall act accordingly until a President or Vice President shall have qualified.

Section 4. The Congress may by law provide for the case of the death of any of the persons from whom the House of Representatives may choose a President whenever the right of choice shall have devolved upon them, and for the case of the death of any of the persons from whom the Senate may choose a Vice President whenever the right of choice shall have devolved upon them.

Section 5. Sections 1 and 2 shall take effect on the 15th day of October following the ratification of this article.

Section 6. This article shall be inoperative unless it shall have been ratified as an amendment to the Constitution by the legislatures of three-fourths of the several States within seven years from the date of its submission.

ARTICLE [XXI]

Section 1. The eighteenth article of amendment to the Constitution of the United States is hereby repealed.

Section 2. The transportation or importation into any State, Territory, or possession of the United States for delivery or use therein of intoxicating liquors, in violation of the laws thereof, is hereby prohibited.

SECTION 3. This article shall be inoperative unless it shall have been ratified as an amendment to the Constitution by conventions in the several States, as provided in the Constitution, within seven years from the date of the submission hereof to the States by the Congress.

ARTICLE [XXII]

SECTION 1. No person shall be elected to the office of the President more than twice, and no person who has held the office of President, or acted as President, for more than two years of a term to which some other person was elected President shall be elected to the office of the President more than once. But this Article shall not apply to any person holding the office of President when this Article was proposed by the Congress, and shall not prevent any person who may be holding the office of President, or acting as President, during the term within which this Article becomes operative from holding the office of President or acting as President during the remainder of such term.

SECTION 2. This article shall be inoperative unless it shall have been ratified as an amendment to the Constitution by the legislatures of three-fourths of the several States within seven years from the date of its submission to the States by the Congress.

ARTICLE [XXIII]

SECTION 1. The District constituting the seat of Government of the United States shall appoint in such manner as the Congress may direct:

A number of electors of President and Vice President equal to the whole number of Senators and Representatives in Congress to which the District would be entitled if it were a State, but in no event more than the least populous State; they shall be in addition to those appointed by the States, but they shall be considered, for the purposes of the election of President and Vice President, to be electors appointed by a State; and they shall meet in the District and perform such duties as provided by the twelfth article of amendment.

SECTION 2. The Congress shall have power to enforce this article by appropriate legislation.

ARTICLE [XXIV]

SECTION 1. The right of citizens of the United States to vote in any primary or other election for President or Vice President, for electors for President or Vice President, or for Senator or Representative in Congress, shall not be denied or abridged by the United States or any State by reason of failure to pay any poll tax or other tax.

SEC. 2. The Congress shall have power to enforce this article by appropriate legislation.

ARTICLE [XXV]

SECTION 1. In case of the removal of the President from office or of his death or resignation, the Vice President shall become President.

SEC. 2. Whenever there is a vacancy in the office of the Vice President, the

President shall nominate a Vice President who shall take office upon confirmation by a majority vote of both Houses of Congress.

SEC. 3. Whenever the President transmits to the President pro tempore of the Senate and the Speaker of the House of Representatives his written declaration that he is unable to discharge the powers and duties of his office, and until he transmits to them a written declaration to the contrary, such powers and duties shall be discharged by the Vice President as Acting President.

SEC. 4. Whenever the Vice President and a majority of either the principal officers of the executive departments or of such other body as Congress may by law provide, transmit to the President pro tempore of the Senate and the Speaker of the House of Representatives their written declaration that the President is unable to discharge the powers and duties of his office, the Vice President shall immediately assume the powers and duties of the office as Acting President.

Thereafter, when the President transmits to the President pro tempore of the Senate and the Speaker of the House of Representatives his written declaration that no inability exists, he shall resume the powers and duties of his office unless the Vice President and a majority of either the principal officers of the executive department or of such other body as Congress may by law provide, transmit within four days to the President pro tempore of the Senate and the Speaker of the House of Representatives their written declaration that the President is unable to discharge the powers and duties of his office. Thereupon Congress shall decide the issue, assembling within forty-eight hours for that purpose if not in session. If the Congress, within twenty-one days after receipt of the latter written declaration, or, if Congress is not in session, within twenty-one days after Congress is required to assemble, determines by two-thirds vote of both Houses that the President is unable to discharge the powers and duties of his office, the Vice President shall continue to discharge the same as Acting President; otherwise, the President shall resume the powers and duties of his office.

Index